Praise for *Unfolding*

"Nancy Hill's writing is intriguing and obviously needed as much for men as the women of our world—if not more."

–Joseph Chilton Pearce, bestselling author of *The Crack in the Cosmic Egg* and *The Biology of Transcendence*

"Nancy Hill's *Unfolding* is a life-changing book that readers will return to again and again. I can't wait to get it in their hands."

–Kathleen March, Anderson's Bookshop, Downers Grove, Illinois

"Reading *Unfolding* is like enjoying a fine piece of chocolate—totally satisfying. Beautifully written, intimate, and engaging, Nancy's book speaks directly to us as women. It draws us in, stimulates our senses, and challenges our thinking. It's all a good book should be, including a catalyst to change our lives. Give it to every woman you know and love."

–Robin A. Sheerer, author of *No More Blue Mondays: Four Keys to Finding Fulfillment at Work*

Unfolding

I want to unfold. I don't want to stay folded anywhere,
because where I am folded, I am untrue.
Rainer Maria Rilke, from *The Book of Hours*

Slow Down,
Drop In,
Dare More

Unfolding

NANCY J. HILL

White Cloud Press titles may be purchased for educational, business, or sales promotional use. For information, please write:

Special Market Department
White Cloud Press
PO Box 3400, Ashland, OR 97520
Website: www.whitecloudpress.com

Cover and interior design by Confluence Book Services
Illustrations on page 20 and 107 by Jessica Cayer Bouchard/ Peapod Arts; on page 48, 65, and mermaid images throughout the book by Taylor Hill; on page 74 by Jennifer Nelson; and on page 116, by Nicola Barsaleau; on page 125 by Jenny Anderson/WunderWalls.

Printed in the United States of America

13 14 15 16 17   10 9 8 7 6 5 4 3 2 1

Library of Congress Cataloging-in-Publication Data

Hill, Nancy J.
  Unfolding : slow down, drop in, dare more / by Nancy J. Hill, LCSW.
    pages cm
  ISBN 978-1-935952-68-8 (pbk.)
  1. Listening. 2. Attention. 3. Conduct of life. I. Title.
  BF323.L5H55 2013
  158--dc23
                                    2013006311

Dedicated to our four granddaughters
Eliana, Taylor, Lillian, Reese
And the unfolding woman in each of their hearts

Contents

Foreword

by Oriah Mountain Dreamer

eading *Unfolding* left me a little in awe of Nancy Hill. Really! I read a lot, and it's not often that an author writes something—particularly something true—that takes my breath away. I expected *Unfolding* to be insightful; I expected it to be full of useful wisdom; I expected it to be well-written and honest. It was all of these. But what I didn't expect was to be truly surprised and deeply inspired, not only by Nancy's wisdom, but by her life, by the way she has embodied the wisdom she has acquired by truly daring to live more than she was taught to expect and far more than what was supported and espoused by the culture around her.

I'm not a big fan of what I call "cheerleading spirituality," the loud and enthusiastic, ever-marketable, slogan-ridden self-improvement programs and promises that urge a weary population to do more, be more, have more, try harder, work faster, and generally be "better" than they are currently. So when I first saw Nancy's website titled "Dare More," I was cautious.

But then I met Nancy. Having been introduced by our now mutual literary agent, Joe, Nancy and I had lunch together on one of my trips to Chicago. And all my misgivings were swept away in the tide of her straightforward, grounded, compassionate sharing. It was like meeting an old girlfriend and a wise elder all rolled into one. We talked about everything from the spiritual meaning of living a human life to the question of whether or not to color our hair. Yes, finding and living from our spiritual center is important, and we both know it is not unrelated to how we live the details of our lives. Leaning toward each other over a café table we considered: Just where is the line between aging gracefully and giving up, between going into denial about and fighting the natural process of aging and simply taking care of ourselves? In that first meeting we shared our questions, our struggles, our momentary successes, and our less-than-fleeting failures to live up to our own ideals when we encountered the reality of an ordinary woman's life.

Lengthy periodic telephone conversations followed over the next few years, and as our conversations deepened I looked forward to reading the book you are now holding in your hands. By then I knew that when Nancy used the term "dare more," she wasn't just talking about living a life of more external adventures and material rewards (although these may come); she was challenging and supporting herself and the rest of us to dig a little deeper, to live closer to the bone of our own truth, guided by values of heart and soul.

As luck (or whatever other unseen forces may benevolently watch over us) would have it, I read *Unfolding* at a crossroads in my own life, in a momentary pause at the end of one year and the beginning of the next. My marriage of the previous decade had disintegrated, my parents were both struggling with Alzheimer's, and my own chronic health challenges seemed to be getting worse. I needed to figure out (once again) what I wanted to do with the next part of my life. The desire to continue writing was there but so too was anxiety about finding a more secure way to pay my rent. It was a perfect time to read Nancy's reminder in *Unfolding* that "The first half of life is about putting ourselves together. The second half is about coming undone. Unwound. Unravelled." This deepened my acceptance of the unravelling that had occurred in my life. I knew that continuing to write was important, but my desire to take new risks in my creative work was reinforced by Nancy's contention that "creativity is far more than making things. It is a stance—a lifestyle with restlessness as a vital part of its cycle. " Relieved to be so eloquently reminded that I did not have to get rid of my own restlessness or see it as a failure to find some idealized state of continuous equanimity, I read on, encouraged to consider the choices that would, as Nancy writes, help me slow down, drop in, and dare more.

But none of this would have had the impact it did—feeding the fire of wanting to "dare more" in this next chapter of my life— without Nancy's story of how she had done just that repeatedly in her own life. She tells these stories without pretension, without claiming to have a formula for "success" by any criteria beyond opening to and following our deepest inner knowing. I'm not going to give away the details here, but I can say I am in awe of how this woman has consistently found her way back to the willingness and courage to act on her own inner knowing, even when those actions were disapproved of by many and changed the shape of the life she shared with her husband and children. Her willingness and ability to ask for and co-create mutual support so that all family members are able to live true to themselves is perhaps the most inspiring part of her work. Working with hundreds of women over the years, I have seen how our ideas about what it means to be Wife and Mother often leave us unable to open to new ways of seeing and living our deepest soul's desires without leaving any aspect of ourselves or those we love behind. Nancy's willingness to wrestle with both the idealized notions and practical details of what it means to be a woman in the world renews my faith in the human spirit.

And at the end of the day—particularly when the day has been one of unravelling—faith is what carries us. We are, each of us, an expression of the sacred life force, whatever we choose to call that mysterious Wholeness that defies definition. Nancy Hill's stories and insights reminded me that I can trust the wisdom that comes from the center of my being because I am—we are—made of and an aspect of that sacred Wholeness. And for that, I am deeply grateful.

Introduction

Doorways: *Entering the Mystery*

Knob in hand.
It turns.
I push.
The door opens.
I enter—
My studio
Womb
Cave
Hidden realm.
I listen—to remember.

*T*here are women who came before, sat to write, stood to paint, stretched to dance, cleared their throats, and spoke. They, like you, wanted to discover the stories deep in their bones. Magic came through their pages, canvases, feet, and voices. They created doorways for us to enter our stories—openings to life's mysteries.

Each of these women, in their own way, tells us to seek solitude for a week, a day, or ten minutes. At times, we are lucky to have just a corner of our bedroom to call our own. Some women take part of a closet and create a spot to think, pray, or meditate. Others use their bathtub to soak in silence.

There are places inside of us we must travel to alone.

Some of us will use painting, writing, or dancing to find these unexplored places. Others will manage employees, care for sick patients, or design tall buildings. There are many entrance points to our souls. What we do will vary. What doesn't vary is a willingness to survey our strengths and weaknesses in the service of self-exploration. Unearthing who we are is an ongoing process. In my sixth decade, I can say with certainty it takes a lot of digging.

Listening to other women we find courage. Seeing how they dared we feel stronger. They take a stand and we are proud. Their examples make us want to speak with passion. We long to give shape to the mystery that moves through us.

Speaking up is risky. It may entail looking foolish. We'll also confront pain and disappointment. Yet when there is harmony between what we experience and how we live, peace settles into our bones. Only through searching our own souls do we find our voice. Only by speaking do we recognize its resonance. Only by acting do we see it manifest in the world.

If I get a tattoo it will be six words inked across my arm—in **BOLD** letters—**Slow Down. Drop In. Dare More**. Then I'd tattoo them on every woman I know. Or better still, I'd put them on my forehead for all to see. Why? We need to hear them. I need to hear them. The messages in this book run counter to our "hurry up, look over here, and don't risk too much" world.

Slow Down—Drop In—Dare More—is a six-word mantra that returns me to me. When we remember these six words our focus shifts. A subtle inner voice arises. Unexpected opportunities appear. We dare to do things we never thought we would.

Slow Down is such a counterculture idea I might be arrested for saying it. Speed and success are hermetically linked. Busyness is now a badge of importance. People run around like their hair is on fire. Some days that describes me. But pausing for even a few minutes of meditation, quiet reflection, or prayer shifts perspective. It takes practice. It can be done. Sometimes it's as simple as taking three deep breaths. Slowing down raises our appreciation for nature, loved ones, and ourselves.

Slowing down ... opens us.

Drop In to excavate the soul. That means embracing all of who we are. Living in the moment should be blissful. Right? Yet sometimes when we drop in we encounter uneasiness. We'd like to be present but without the risk of feeling discomfort. Intuitively we know that isn't possible. Fearing what we'll find makes us reluctant to *drop in*. It keeps us running.

We avoid silence. The noise of TV or iPods keeps us distracted. Dropping in requires a willingness to be present to our total experience. It's how we discover who we are—right now. In middle adulthood our awareness turns from *out there* to *in here*. That takes boldness and compassion. It takes practice. The willingness to embrace who we are links us to our soul.

Dropping in … connects us.

Dare More is not about having more or doing more. Soulless daring is not satisfying. It leaves us drained of meaning. The desire for meaning grows in importance as we age. Interests we dismissed in our youth return. Forgotten dreams call again. Do we listen now? It takes audacity to resist the urge to settle into complacency. It requires repeated leaps into the unknown. Courageous choices that proclaim our essence are both risky and rewarding.

Daring more … reveals us.

⸻

This August morning I am sitting on our porch. Pewter-colored clouds float slowly to the east. Treetops are still. I am still. Growling truck sounds come from a nearby construction site. Their racket is an odd contrast to the perky tweets of sparrows and chickadees.

Slap goes my neighbors' newspaper on their driveway. News of the world can arrive that way, all tidy and organized. It can come by the expression of other women's lives. Or it can drift into us on a quiet morning.

Mother Nature also delivers news. When she speaks we are not distant observers. She gently and powerfully pulls us back to our sense of wonder. Listening to her we know that our cells are alive with the same energy that runs through a sparrow or a blade of grass.

Mother Nature's big news…you *are* an unfolding Mystery!

This is my wish for you:

Slow Down and open to the once-only expression of life that you are. *Drop In* and connect with the complexity and intensity that you hold. *Dare More* and unfold your true self.

Hummingbird

Tugging on Invisible Cords

*When we try to pick out anything by itself, we find it
hitched to everything else in the Universe.*
John Muir, from *My First Summer in the Sierra*

*S*low down is not on my list of errands. But this day, note in hand, I stop in my tracks. A hummingbird catches my eye. Suspended in midair she laps up nectar from the deep-throated foxglove outside the dining room window. I freeze.

Scribbled list in hand…

Pick up meds.

Drop off dry cleaning.

Return library books.

I add, *Buy hummingbird feeder.*

1

The lady at the Wild Bird Store instructs me to place this right where I saw the bird. It makes sense. All the flowers that attract hummers—foxglove, delphinium, and wisteria—grow there. But I work looking out a different window, where only hydrangeas are in view. It's not their favorite dining spot.

Still, I hope these perpetually hungry birds, who eat as much as their own body weight every day, are also curious. Maybe they'll notice my new feeder. It's a globe of blue glass, the color of a Noxzema jar. Red flower-shaped openings let birds slurp up sugary water. Every few seconds or so, I check to see if any teaspoon-sized consumers have found their treat. What is that at the edge of my field of vision? A white butterfly teasingly grabs my attention. Do I have a customer? Not yet. All three seats remain open for business.

Waiting.

Expectant.

Longing.

Days have gone by with no sign of what famous birdwatcher John Audubon called "a glittering fragment of the rainbow." I continue to change the food every four days or so and wait. Now the feeder hangs on the porch. I can see it from my desk. It's still not where the bird first appeared. That human desire to mold nature to our will is strong in me.

Reading about the life and habits of hummingbirds, I discover the hummingbird moth. It is often mistaken for a hummingbird.

Doubt raises its ugly head.

Did I see a hummingbird impostor?

Christopher Columbus, sailing in 1493 near what we now call the Dominican Republic, wrote in his log that he spotted mermaids… "female forms … rose high out of the sea, but were not as beautiful as they are represented." Many are convinced he saw manatees, not mystical maidens. How much wine would he need to have swallowed to confuse one for the other? Rum was not yet the sailors' drink of choice. Columbus brought that about later by introducing sugarcane to the islands. It is true that alcohol, loneliness, and longing can do crazy things to optic nerves. While I do long to spot hummers, I hadn't had a drop of wine or rum that morning.

Disbelief shades my enthusiasm. It tones it down. Verifying my sighting is reasonable. Yet my desire for proof reminds me of what happens to us as children. There is such joy in discovering the world. Curiosity is childhood's natural state. We want to see everything and know how it works. We love to ask questions and persist until our parents clamp hands over their ears and beg us to stop. Carl Sagan, Cornell astronomer and science advocate, said that children are the only ones who are not afraid to ask big questions: Why is the sky blue and the grass green? If the world is spinning why don't we fall off? Where did we come from? Are we alone in the universe?

At some point, most of us quit asking.

What we knew as children is that … Life unfolds. We unfold. We sensed it when our shoes came off in the spring and cool damp earth met the bottoms of our feet. We felt it when the first snowflake melted on our warm nose. Cracks in the sidewalk opened to a universe of small beings called ants. Prodding and poking our surroundings we noticed that everything had layers. Everything was a happening.

Ironically, scientists speak with that same childlike wonder as they peer into the depths of the universe. Einstein said, "The most beautiful thing we can experience is the mysterious. It is the source of all true art and all science. He to whom this emotion is a stranger, who can no longer pause to wonder and stand rapt in awe, is as good as dead: his eyes are closed." Something happens as we mature. Curiosity dies. We cease asking questions. Intuitively, we realize there is something happening that no one can explain. Part of the problem is the way we speak of our experience.

Language seems neutral. It's merely a way to communicate. But it also *shapes* and *reflects* our worldview. David Bohm was a physicist, author, philosopher and original thinker. He described how the laws of language distort reality: "Language imposes strong, subtle pressures to see the world as fragmented and static." Language is like a lifesaving medicine with negative side effects. We need it so much that its consequences become irrelevant. But the influence of language on perception is profound. It often removes us from our direct experience of the world.

The way we form nouns and verbs divides the world into *things* and *actions*. In reality, everything is dynamic. Everything is a process. Bohm said that there are "fast verbs," like walking, and "slow verbs," like tables. The antique table where I work is made of oak trees that once were acorns, seedlings, saplings, trees, then lumber, then finished wood, then a table. In this very moment my table is changing. Someday it will become rubbish and compost. Eventually it will return to dust. It is slowly transforming. Bohm said it is more accurate to say it's "table-ing." It's not a static noun, a thing we call "table." It is an event.

It's unfolding.

———

I'm renting a flat with other women while I'm here in San Francisco. Basically, it's a place to sleep after long days in a one-week "process painting" workshop. It's a method of self-discovery that enhances intuition and spontaneity by focusing on the painter rather than resulting painting. We learn to connect with our creative "voice" while letting go of the need for approval and perfection. Images emerge that have unique meaning for us as we struggle to stay present. The work is intense and surprisingly tiring. I'm exhausted. Focus takes energy.

Our rooms—two bedrooms, kitchen, and bathroom—are sparsely furnished. We are on the second floor, down a long hallway where the wainscoting, floors, and stairs are painted institutional gray. The lively neighborhood of North Beach, nestled between Chinatown and Fishermen's Wharf, makes up for all that is missing in the decor.

This building was once a boarding house; now it accommodates travelers who are looking for location, not luxury. It was likely built after the 1906 earthquake. Few structures remained after the fires that followed the shaking. Perched on one of the many hilly San Francisco streets, it leans downhill at a pronounced angle. The stairways that run from floor to floor slant. Moving up or down is tricky. I sit writing on steps that lead to the roof—here I am away from the chatter in our flat.

Not only does the staircase tilt, but the foot-worn steps dip in the middle. Countless soles have fashioned a concave groove in what must once have been a smooth surface. In this silence, I feel the presence of those who trod up and down where I now sit. Did they notice how their movements left these marks? Could they imagine that more than one hundred years later a woman would wonder about their lives? Doubtful. There is a wispy feeling here, like the afterglow that remains following a friend's visit. Something lingers.

Children's laughter. A woman's muffled voice. A man shouts, "Where's my dinner?" Silence. Slam goes the screen door. Bang goes the skillet. Soundless tears streak her cheeks.

Gingerly, a soon-to-be mother heads downstairs. Shudders of labor overcome her. She stops. The cold, clammy hands of her young husband reach out to steady her bulky body.

Imprinted in paint and plaster are the bits and pieces of their stories.

It is easy to see that structures come and go, to see leaning buildings as part of the natural changes that occur. We accept that they are not permanent. We can see that others have lived here with their stories, hopes, and dreams. But our own impermanence is hard to grasp. We are moving through life and life is moving through us.

We cannot stop it.

By midlife we have discovered that we are not in control—even the things we care about most, we are not able rule. Husbands, children, grandchildren, clients, even bad habits are not changed by our willing it so. It is hard to live with that truth. It's really difficult for me because I want to manage things…well, most things…like where the hummingbirds choose to feed. But the longer I live the more I realize this obvious truth: I am not in charge.

In August, the burning bush at the west end of the porch is brushed with shades of crimson. It announces the coming changes. Fussy wisteria no longer has flowers dripping from its vines. Foxglove that bloomed in early summer is now just stalks, leaves, and seedpods. Indigo delphinium's latest bloom found its way to the center of a summer bouquet in my kitchen. Soon, it too will cease flowering.

I finally give up and move the hummingbird feeder to where I first saw that mystical mite of a bird. I was stubborn. I hope that Hummer hasn't given up on me. But there is little chance of seeing it now. This I can promise: When my garden awakens from her winter's nap, I know right where I'll place that feeder. It will hang wherever the Hummingbird wants to dine.

Mid-September I spot a dead field mouse on our back porch. I want to give it a dignified burial, but it's suppertime. I can't bring myself to stop and pick it up. Dinner and dead mice just don't go together. So I tell myself the morning will have to do. I know an animal might eat it tonight, but I plan a morning funeral—if it is still there.

In the morning, the little critter is still lying just outside the door. I scoop her up and dig a hole next to the walkway where the lavender grows. Fallen rose petals are nearby so I add them. Then I remember incense ashes in the hall. I bring them out to sprinkle over the flowers. I close the grave and put a football-sized stone over it. It will keep the visiting cats from unearthing her.

It is a small act of kindness, of reverence for life. It is and isn't only about the mouse. These creatures have been unwelcome guests in my kitchen. And I've been responsible for killing them in the past. It is not that I'd never hurt a flea. But this creature touches some place in me. A place that says life is not cheap…even the life of a mouse counts. As I step away I think, *I have returned you to the mystery from which we all come.*

Filling the fountain in the front yard, I imagine the dark earth ready to gobble mouse flesh and bones. In that very moment my prized visitor, the magical hummingbird, returns. She flies next to my head about two feet away and just hovers so I can get a good look.

Then she is gone.

Thank you. Thank you, I say. *All summer I've waited, moved the feeder, changed the food and nothing. I doubted if I'd really seen you. Now, as if a blessing, you appear.* Tugging on one part of nature I connect to everything. Life is unfolding. We don't need to learn how to unfold.

It happens.

We just have to recognize it.

Life flows through us the way water pours through a waterfall. Water flows. The shape remains. We are like the curve of the waterfall. This is what I am discovering again and again. To hold this truth lets us see what we saw as children.

Life IS a dance of energy.

There is a great mystery that we can glimpse moving through life—through everything—through us. How do we encounter it? Slow down, to notice it. Drop in, to fully experience it. Dare more, and say what we see. That is how this great mystery becomes real. It is how we start to see again.

With this vision the simplest things become sacred.

Mermaid

Soul Spotting

You use a glass mirror to see your face; you use works of art to see your soul.
George Bernard Shaw

Our soul is always flirting with us.

My eyes drift around the room. Then I spot her—a life-size mermaid painting hanging on a wall just a few feet away. Patchy colors of aqua, teal, and gold illuminate her. She's captivating. I'm not sure why. Don, my husband, and his father are talking about the Chicago Bears. Their hopeful voices are barely audible in the midst of this noisy restaurant. They sound like amnesiacs to me. Don't they recall decades of disappointing defeats? I do. I catch up on family news, especially about our four granddaughters, with Don's mom.

When coffee topped with frothy milk arrives, the four of us seamlessly transition from football and family chatter to beginning our goodbyes. But I'm still distracted. I keep glancing back at the mermaid.

Something continues to draw me to her.

Floating on her side in a blue-green sea, she glides in a state of reverie. Blonde hair flows around her shoulders. Turquoise scales. Milk-white skin. Eyes gently closed. She holds me spellbound. Provocative. Poised. Playful. "Follow me," she says.

For days after my mermaid encounter, I spend way too much time researching mermaids. My glassy eyes are glued to Google as I click through many of the six million references. Something unexplainable about these goddesses of the deep is important to me. I am determined to figure out why. I buy books, watch mermaid movies, read research articles, visit blogs, and exhaust myself.

Mermaids are everywhere I turn.

They swim across labels of tuna fish and full-page ads for plumbing supplies. Burger, beer, and ice cream commercials use these seductresses to attract buyers. Ads for Coke Zero, Pop Tarts, Clorox, and Capital One cards feature them. They frequent paintings, poems, movies, and bedtime stories. SpongeBob episodes include them. Superman, man of steel, fell in love with one. Smiling from the Starbucks logo, they seem to be on every corner. Even in the dark seas of sleep, I see mermaids.

Hunches confound the thinking mind. But they have the ring of truth to our souls. As a psychotherapist, I've learned that these longings can seem, well, crazy. We try to make them fit with life as we know it. But they are unsettling. That is the point. Their job is to unearth aspects of us that are buried, forgotten, or never celebrated. I work with clients to help them understand their own intuitive nudges. Paying attention to these niggling tugs often pays off with renewed energy and a fuller sense of one's gifts and talents. Knowing this didn't stop me from wondering if I should move on and leave these fishy women alone. To tell you the truth, I couldn't.

Although something as fringey as a mermaid may not grab everyone, each of us has chambers in our soul that long for discovery. When we start this exploration there are things to consider. Do we listen to the whisper of intuition or look a little saner and ignore it? Should we align our life with what the world wants from us? Or do we take the messier and more unpredictable path that hopefully delivers us to our true self? That self takes its marching orders from inside. Radical trust is what we need at times like these, when we rely on an inner sense to direct us, without knowing where we are headed. That sounds difficult. It is.

The soul speaks a strange language of images, inklings, and feelings. Its messages are often ambiguous. It doesn't offer clear steps; it's more like a come-hither look. To follow it seems like trusting a Magic Eight Ball rather than a Rand McNally map. But I'll offer a testimonial here—a glowing endorsement. It is worth the struggles and the turmoil that you'll surely encounter. We each have to trust our longings without knowing what we'll face or where we'll arrive.

Confront the rational mind with intuitive discoveries and it will search for the proper brain file. We have a scrupulous inner file clerk living in our heads. Her guiding principle is tidiness. Sorting is her game. Risky yearnings are the bane of her existence. Her motto: Maintain the Status Quo. I could see her standing, hands on hips, warning me: "Intuition invites messiness!" She was determined to file away mermaids—to dismiss them. My fussy file clerk seemed locked in a tug-of-war with my soul. I was caught between caution and exuberance—abandon and appropriateness. Yet some part of me refused to accept that my mermaid fascination was insignificant.

I wanted to be immersed in her.

What would it be like to make a life-sized mermaid, I wonder? Closing my eyes, I picture a mermaid collage. *But to do this I'd be cutting up magazines for weeks.* Then I imagine her made of papier-mâché. *Too messy, and where on earth will I put a mermaid that big?* Both ideas seem overwhelming and time-consuming. Painting is my answer. Even though I have little experience, I know this is what I need to do.

This is where the story takes an unexpected twist—the kind Carl Jung, renowned Swiss psychiatrist, called "meaningful coincidences." Many of us have made what we think is a wrong choice only to see later that it was actually a fortunate mistake. Or there is the book that comes to us by chance that contains just the information we wanted. Meaningful coincidences are like that. They're seemingly random actions that take us right where we need to go. We are often blithely unaware of our inevitable destination. But looking back, we see an unfaltering path that leads right to our dusty soul.

Life is a game of hide-and-seek played with our soul.

The trick is to notice we're being tagged.

Our soul is always flirting with us. A profound connection to the story we're living is ours for the taking. As James Hollis says in *Finding Meaning in the Second Half of Life,* "We are always in the presence of the soul, whether consciousness reflects it or not." We have to come out of hiding to discover our essence. It means spending time with difficult questions that take us to unfamiliar places. Questions like… What do I value? When do I feel most alive? It takes getting off the highway and dropping into a hammock long enough to notice the way sunlight filters through the trees. Ironically, tuning in to our five senses links us to our souls. Better still, being present to what we encounter in the moment releases us from the race to nowhere. This all takes some doing in the world that we now inhabit.

Glazed eyeballs slide over dozens of emails. Silence is an endangered experience. We wear busyness as a badge of importance. Is it any wonder we don't feel the soul's tug, hear her whisper, or catch a glimpse of her as she beckons? A great mystery lives within us. It sits with us as we flip from channel to channel. It watches as we scoop ice cream from the freezer. It stares as we pour another glass of wine. It leans against the sink as we brush our teeth, waiting and wondering—when will we notice?

And while we could feel the soul's tap at any moment, it is more likely to occur in the second half of life. The first half of life is about putting ourselves together. The second half is about coming undone. Unwound. Unraveled. For many of us, this is when we tire of the life we've inherited or constructed. We realize that it is no longer nourishing. It served a particular phase and often reflects what we needed or thought we needed as a younger woman. But now we are different. We want to inhabit this difference by being fully us. When we realize this, bindings that once held us in place begin to let go like the frayed laces of an old corset.

The desire to be more fully ourselves often begins with a growing restlessness. This disquiet looks like the problem. But it's an invitation. Until we realize that, our focus is on trying to rid ourselves of the distress. Like a bout of indigestion, we'll take something that will make it go away—now. In an attempt to snap out of it, we search for the usual reassuring cures. Could it be that I need a new hairstyle? Does the bedroom need a fresh coat of paint? Should I try a new career? If the alterations are only on the surface the unrest remains. I can testify to this because I tried all three. Each one brought some relief. But my uneasiness continued.

Before that night in the restaurant, I'd already changed my hairstyle, rehabbed the house, and switched the focus of my profession. I left a position on the medical staff of a psychiatric hospital and closed my psychotherapy office. My work shifted from working with individuals to leading workshops and women's groups. These were satisfying changes. But I needed to make an inner shift.

With bold, childlike strokes the mermaid tumbles out of me and lands on six large sheets of paper. I step back and expect an "Aha!" moment, like a payout from some celestial slot machine. It doesn't happen.

Of course my inner file clerk has so much to say. *You don't know how to paint. Are you doing this right? This looks crazy.* Spontaneous expression happens when she takes a nap. With her out of the way it's easier to move. The process painting teacher helped me stay in the flow of painting and out of my judgments. After a few sessions, I began to notice a change in awareness from "out there" to an interior reference point. It felt foreign and delightful.

I often lead with my head. I like to examine the outcome of an action before I take the next step. It feels less risky. Painting gave me a deeper appreciation of intuition. Scrutinizing inklings takes the life out of them. We have to trace over them with our senses. Taste them like nectar. Dance with them.

Hydrangea bushes snuggle up to the northwest corner of our house. They are visible from the family room where I sit and write. With winter's approach they're becoming a coppery brown. Fragile gray shadows of their former selves will appear in March. Chicago's winds will toss them this way and that until they nearly disappear. In May, they return as clusters of pale green petals and in summer's fullness turn a brilliant white. Slender stems are then no match for the weight of their flowery heads. Like dutiful subjects, they bow to the ground.

Now dry and papery they stand bravely upright. Season after season, I watch something mysterious yet predictable cycle through my garden. Its movement reminds me of what the Welsh poet Dylan Thomas called "the force that through the green fuse drives the flower." I trace it by the changes I see in my garden and in my life. I can't understand this mystery by doing a Google search. Neither can I explain my mermaid encounter by researching. Invisible forces move through us and around us. They can be experienced but not explained.

My mermaid fascination is teaching me some valuable lessons. Life is not a product to be filed and sorted, but a process to behold. Living with this awareness feeds the soul. Sometimes, regardless of what the inner file clerk says, we have to make a mess in order to free ourselves. We have to trust what nature shows us.

Life unfolds.

Ancient sages looked up at the Milky Way and pictured a progression of souls ascending and descending. While this is a beautiful image, one that I love, it can be misleading. Embracing our soul isn't about gliding into a light-filled apparition. It's welcoming all of who we are. Can I accept my grouchiness that comes out as impatient nipping? Will I love the judgmental part of me that looks for faults in women who are prettier and more successful? Do I have compassion for the part of me that wants my children's lives to make me look like a perfect mother?

What about embracing my pesky file clerk? It was a mistake to put her in charge of too much of my life. Clearly, she is a good employee but a restrictive boss. Her skills of implementation and coordination are remarkable. That is our work as humans, to do the best we can and acknowledge there will always be gaps. We don't become a perfect rendition but an authentic expression of ourselves. We are called to celebrate our eccentric, less than perfect, human selves.

Teachers like Socrates taught that we were sent into this world knowing why we were born and what gifts we came to share. I wonder if that means we receive instructions something like these... *This is your job, if you choose to take this earth assignment. Get to know yourself. Use your gifts. Reveal who you are. Discover that we are all connected. See you back here when your time is up. By the way, help others. They are trying to do the same thing.* According to some, whatever instructions we receive disappear during the trauma of birth.

We forget.

The soul remembers.

It's always nudging us toward that memory of who we are.

However we arrive, there are challenges to remembering what gifts we have to share. Trials come at predictable points throughout our lives. I'd been leading the women's groups for years before I realized that all the members, including me, fell into what developmental psychologist Erik Erikson called "Middle Adulthood"—the ages of thirty-five to sixty-five. In that period we choose either to stagnate or generate. In the second half of life the inevitable test is... *Will we struggle to maintain where we are—or—will we create a life that reflects who we are becoming?*

After painting in the local art studio for a couple of months, I began traveling to workshops taught by Michele Cassou, origina-tor of the process. Eventually she invited me to become one of her apprentices. Being a trainee in my late fifties was odd. But I ac-cepted. By saying yes, I shifted from protection of my professional status to a riskier path of self-discovery. In truth, I was apprenticing my own inner tug as much as to Michele's method. I didn't see that then. Now I do.

We are free when we shift from finding the right answer "out there" to staying attentive to an unfolding inner direction. A stronger connection to intuition emerges with this change in focus. Susan Griffin reflected this budding awareness in *Thoughts on Writing*: "But still, the other voice, the intuitive, returns, like grass forcing its way through concrete." Many of us long to let inner guidance have a larger role in our choices, especially in the second half of our lives. We want to trust our inner authority and speak from there with boldness and compassion.

We need places and people that help us delve into these questions. Painting and the women's groups are where I do my exploring. I laugh sometimes and say that the groups are really voice lessons. Not the singing kind, but the ones where we practice speaking authentically. It's where we honor who we have been and are faithful to our emerging self. Both painting and the women's groups help develop a keen inner listening. Without that, it's easy to get stuck in the noisy chorus we call our minds.

People-pleasing and perfectionism often drown out the softer tones of authenticity and acceptance. I wish self-doubt disappeared. But it hasn't for my clients or me. However, we can learn to recognize its downer messages. If we're tuned into self-doubt, enthusiasm diminishes, our energy drops, and stopping sounds sensible. The way to escape this cycle is to notice which voice is whispering to us. We can notice if our energy drops or rises. If we're feeling increasingly apathetic, we need to make a shift. We can learn to do as author Anne Sexton says: "Put your ear down close to your soul and listen hard."

Slippery mermaids continue to appear in unexpected places. Can I explain my captivation with them? No. That is part of their delight. Why do people spend hours and money creating model railroad scenes as Don is now doing? He finds joy and satisfaction in it. I see it in his eyes. I've studied mermaid myths and searched my psyche to understand why they grabbed me. The inner file clerk would love an explanation. I love leaving them shrouded in mystery.

Mermaids are my muses. Ambiguous. Seductive. They are how my soul flirts with me. The other day I saw a cinnamon-haired, full-breasted beauty painted on the bathroom door of our local Trader Joe's store. She reminded me that boldness and quirkiness can save me from the inner file clerk's clutches. The world needs our full-throated contribution to its choir. It's essential that we sing out—even when it makes others uncomfortable, even when it makes us uncomfortable.

Winter's first snowfall arrived last night. Don left for work at 6:30 a.m., his usual departure time. Around 7:30, I awake to that familiar whirring noise of tires spinning on ice. Exhaust fumes drift into the bedroom through the window left ajar for the crisp night air. Reluctantly I get out of bed, close the window, and size up the situation. A woman delivering newspapers had the misfortune to slide off the street at the curve. *Should I get dressed and go out there*, I wonder. That means peeling off these warm pajamas, not a pleasant thought. The whine of her engine continues to call for help.

I've been in that seat. I remember how frustrated and helpless I felt. My foot planted on the accelerator, the car not moving. Like her, the only thing I had to show for my effort was a rut that kept getting deeper. In situations like this, something in us repeats the same action hoping for a different outcome. Stopping means we'll face the discomfort of not knowing what else to do. That "not knowing" is very scary. But in these moments when we are without an answer, intuition has a chance to contact us. Our soul welcomes the unfamiliar. Not knowing gives the soul room to roam. The inner file clerk fears it.

In the few minutes it takes to dress and reach the kitchen, the paper delivery lady disappears. Did her tires finally engage? Did someone pull her car out of the ditch? I don't know. What I do know is that her situation is like many of ours. Pushing the same pedal won't yield a different result. If we pause, if we listen, hidden under the nagging discontent we will hear intuition's soft voice.

That night in the restaurant, looking at the mermaid painting, I listened to something that couldn't be articulated. It took me in a new direction, though my life hasn't changed much on the outside. Significant changes have happened inside of me. My respect for each woman's life as a process with its own timing and wisdom has grown. I see that creativity is far more than making things. It is a stance—a lifestyle with restlessness as a vital part of its cycle. Now I spend less time thinking about where actions will take me and more time moving with intuition as a guide.

If—and it is a big if—if we take a risk and let go of who we think we are, there is an untried and more lively self to discover. Mary Oliver describes this in her poem, "The Journey": "and there was a new voice / which you slowly / recognized as your own." It is like that. Our words start to come from an unfamiliar place and life becomes less certain yet more alive. And over time, we rely on something inside that we haven't trusted for a long time or maybe never. It calls us into deeper waters. Uncertainty fills us. Fear strikes. Energized and uneasy is how we feel on the brink of self-discovery. There is only one thing to do.

Trust it!

Moon

Remembering Essence

*See how nature—trees, flowers, grass—grows in silence; see the stars,
the moon and the sun, how they move in silence...we need
silence to be able to touch souls.*
Mother Teresa

Wake up to your life!
My eyes blink open. 4:00 a.m. spelled out in tiny
red dashes. I am wide awake. It's difficult to ignore a
command like that—no matter how sleepy you are. This cryptic
message, "Wake up to your life!" tugs at me. Like an insistent friend,
it shakes me from slumber. Sends me from my bed. Rousts me
from comfort.

As I slide out from covers warmed by the heat of our bodies,
Don lifts his head. *Are you okay?* I reassure him with a whispered,
Yes, I just can't sleep. The room is dark. I follow the carpeted hallway

to the top of the oak staircase. My bare feet search for one step after another. Once I'm downstairs, the cool wooden floor guides me to our kitchen. Occasionally I awaken early, but this is different. This is a morning like the one Rumi describes:

The breeze at dawn has secrets to tell you.
Don't go back to sleep.
You must ask for what you really want.
Don't go back to sleep.

Some people blame sleep disturbances on a rich dinner or a second glass of wine. That can happen. But spiritual traditions teach us to greet these events as opportunities. They say that early mornings are a propitious time to meditate, write, or sit in silence. Our brain glides on waves of heightened awareness and inspiration before beginning to whir with activity. It's easier to hear the whisper of our soul at dawn. It's as if it says, *I've been trying to get your attention to tell you this. Finally, your mind is quiet enough to hear me. Wake up! Wake up! Don't go back to sleep!*

What does it mean to wake up to your life? I've been curious about this for decades, studied, read, and meditated to understand conscious living. It boils down to landing, with both feet, in the here and now. Once we do, it's clear that there is more going on than we often notice, even though the present moment is the only place we can *ever* be. Surprisingly, it's difficult to locate. Finding it seems urgent. Especially when, as modern day guru Eckhart Tolle says: "Your inner purpose is to awaken. It is as simple as that." It may be simple but that doesn't mean it is easy. It did seem more possible at dawn in a silent house than it did over the last few days.

Our children and grandchildren left last night. The empty kitchen holds traces of our time together: a doll, a sippy cup, splashes on the stove, and leftovers…lots of leftovers. The little handprints that now adorn the window remind me of how their visits touch my life.

Preparations start days before they arrive. With three and sometimes four generations crowded together, fully stocked cabinets are emptied of towels, sheets, and dishes. It is a noisy, busy time. Bless their little cotton socks, our four granddaughters are an energetic lot. Their excitement erupts through the house like a tsunami, leaving me clutching sanity like a coconut clinging to a waving palm tree.

Before they arrive, I picture myself as Lady Bountiful—their needs anticipated and fulfilled with ease. In this fantasy, my kitchen is much bigger than it really is. I never have to ask anyone to move so I can open the refrigerator door. In my actual kitchen, we waltz around each other to the shrieks of a toddler and the banter of brothers-in-law. It is the busiest dance floor in town. My expectations of perfection quickly slip into organized chaos. I begin to feel like Martha Stewart on crack.

In the midst of a cooking frenzy—Kathy chopping potatoes, Deb sautéing something, and me in my usual scurry—eight-year-old Lilly has a question. I stop. She looks up at me with tender brown eyes, a glue stick in her hand. She's ready to create a diorama at—where else—the kitchen table.

"Grandma, which do you like better, fairies or mermaids?"

"Mermaids," I say without hesitation.

When our family is together, I fall into the story of what it means to be a mother and grandmother. Family stories are ancient. We know them well. Their familiarity can put us to sleep and take us out of the moment. But sometimes we see through them. I remember the exact moment when I saw that my mother was just another woman trying to make sense of her life.

It was always obvious, yet my need for her to be a certain way obscured this truth for decades. Like a character in a play, she was so convincing that both the audience and the actor forgot she had another life. Too often, this realization comes after a parent dies. It is then that we discover the heart of the person as we reflect on what brought them joy. Death's gift is the chance to appreciate the spirits of those we love.

Author Joyce Carol Oates used the memory of her grandmother as the basis for a character in *The Gravedigger's Daughter*. In an interview she said, "I did not know her except as a grandmother. She was…I wouldn't say playing a role, because it was very genuine. She was the quintessential grandmother who loved her grandchildren and whose grandchildren loved her, but we never really knew her." Oates found, like so many of us, that the family connections are authentic, but they reveal only a piece of the person.

I love being a grandmother and joyfully embrace this tender relationship. To some extent, my role in the family comes from what I saw as a girl. But it is also spun from what I would want a child to have. I conjured it from the images I saw on TV or in the homes of my friends. I became the grandmother I wanted to have. Yet it becomes tiring if I think I *have* to be a certain way. Agatha Christie, that great creator of characters, knew what it meant to construct exhausting roles. "As life goes on it becomes tiring to keep up the character you've invented for yourself, and so you relapse into individuality and become more like yourself every day. This is sometimes disconcerting for those around you, but a great relief to the person concerned."

Lilly's question broke the family story's spell. Words sent directly from the heart bring us back to the moment. In an instant, I really *saw* her—a little girl who longed to delight me. She finished her shoebox creation as we served dinner. It was complete with cut and colored fish, seaweed, and of course a longhaired sea goddess. Mermaids appeal to most little girls and some grandmothers. They feed our spirits. Love for these daughters of the deep gives me an untraditional bond with my granddaughters. I see it in their eyes.

When we were ready to pass the dessert, a flourless chocolate cake, we discovered that the salad hadn't made it to the table. It was lost in the shuffle. I think if I were really in the moment, I would have remembered to serve the salad. Life is a series of moments where we are aware and then unaware. Our job is to notice the difference.

Now, in dawn's darkness the house is still. Our tiny tribe disbanded. Outside the window, a full Passover moon hangs in the southwest corner of an indigo sky. The Ojibwa medicine wheel says southwest is the direction of hopes and dreams. Recalling this is reassuring—I'm not sure why. I watch as *Our Lady in White* slides behind cedar branches. As she moves, her invisible power pulls oceans from their banks.

Soon this full moon will appear as a lunar slice. But the shape of the moon never really changes. The moon is round—always round. We know this. Earth's silhouette will slip across its surface and transform what we observe. We say, "There is just a sliver of the moon in the sky tonight." Sometimes we don't distinguish between what we see and the truth of what is happening.

The roles we play are similar to phases of the moon. We appear as daughter, sister, wife, mother, or grandmother. In any given moment, our role looks like the whole picture, but it's only a slice of who we are. Essence doesn't change. When we lose sight of this, we create a smaller story about others and ourselves. We become actors with hidden lives. Our actions become mechanical and fragmented. When we remember the undeniable truth of our fullness, we relax into ourselves.

It is so easy to forget.

Intuitively, I know the dance of *alone/together* and *silence/noise* enriches. These aspects fit in some intricate, imperceptible pattern. At times, they seem separate and conflicting. It's as if I'm dancing with two partners doing two different dances. Each partner pulls me in a different direction. One dance draws me to a quiet inner union with myself. The other carries me to outer activities and relationships.

Both deepen my life.

We live in a dynamic tension between turning outward and turning inward. Other. Balance. Self. Caring for others and a desire for reflection make both precious. It's the challenge of every life. Maintaining harmony between our inner and outer connections takes work. First, we must find our way in our parents' world. There we struggle to find a separate, unique voice. Then as partners, employees, or parents we need to locate the "me" in the "we" of relationships.

Recently Reese, our two-year-old granddaughter, fell in love with the moon. Her baby eyes discovered it on a ride home. There hanging in the blue-black sky was a glowing lunar ball. She followed it from our house to theirs. As Kathy tucked her into the crib, she found it again outside her bedroom window. "Moon! Moon!" The next morning she immediately pointed to the window. "Moon? Moon?" It was gone.

Grandchildren and grandparents find it easier than parents to reach around the roles we play. We have different expectations of each other—different ways to connect. At either end of life, there is curiosity and awe. Grandchildren are at the wondrous beginning and grandparents at the wondrous end of life. They see things for the first time. We cherish beauty in the face of impermanence.

We can both risk being in love with the moon.

Our grandchildren's parents are in the middle of busy lives. During that phase it's important to remember what H. G. Wells said: "We must not allow the clock and the calendar to blind us to the fact that each moment of life is a miracle and mystery." Roles of work and family are intense at life's midpoint. Schedules and expectations often shape our days. But it is more than busyness that grips us. In these middle years, we strain against a carefully constructed life as an unnamable restlessness stirs inside of us. If we are fortunate, we will "relapse into individuality."

Outside my window, the moon begins to fade. Sunlight is unfurling fuchsia ruffles at the edges of the clouds. I hear a robin's song. Turquoise eggs, encircled by twigs, hold the promise of another robin. Our pond wiggles with spring's new life. Tadpoles whip from side to side and carry unfolding frogs. And in our hearts, the soul's voice continues to whisper. *Stay awake! Stay awake!*

Red Pepper

Being Here Now

Those who have eyes know just how irrelevant words are to what they see . . .
To define a thing is to substitute the definition for the thing itself.
Georges Braque

*L*ast week I found a red pepper in the dishwasher. There
on the top rack, a green stem pointed straight up at
me. The vegetable shrugged its shoulders in disbelief
to find itself next to my blue coffee mug. I had no explanation.
It waited for me to realize my mistake. Patiently. This Zen master
cloaked in red chanted, "Be here now."

I wasn't "here" when I let the pepper join the ranks of dirty
dishes. Well, all of me wasn't. The analytical part of me made a
quick judgment. The pepper was round, smooth, brightly colored,
and tall as a mug. They were of a similar weight. This gardener's

delight, sitting with dishes on the kitchen counter, was an easy target. My assessment: *Send it to the dishwasher.*

Had I felt its wavy sides, smelled the earthy scent, heard the thud of hollow walls, bitten into pungent flesh, or really seen its crimson skin—I would have known. *This is not a mug.* But my senses were not on duty. My hand, like a robot's, plucked the pepper from the countertop. My inner file clerk, who sorts and orders everything I encounter, is quick—really quick.

I can't remember when my inner file clerk wasn't on duty. I bet she set up shop soon after I learned the alphabet. Reading *The Alphabet Versus the Goddess* by Leonard Shlain makes that seem likely. He says, "Learning to spell occurs at such a young age that people are unaware of the changes in perception that it causes." If he is right, spelling plucks us out of a big picture worldview and shifts us to seeing life as a series of details. Life becomes piles of things to organize.

My inner file clerk, armed with this all-encompassing language system, began to catalogue everything. She is a crazy crafter with a new label gun ready to tag all that she sees. Mug…click…dish… click…spoon…click, click. Everything has a place on the mind's orderly shelves. Yes, she sometimes makes mistakes as she smacks labels on this and that. But she has a system. Is that a bad thing? Yes and no. A world without our ability to categorize knowledge and experience would be chaotic.

Labeling is the core of language. It allows us to order our world. But it also diminishes being in the moment by encouraging us to see all we encounter as "one of these or one of those." We are constantly looking for patterns. By the time we've become adults what we come upon flashes past us to land in its appropriate file. It's so rapid we don't even realize that we are doing it. The problem is, as Simone Weil said, "A mind enclosed in language is in prison."

When we enter its gated walls, it is easier to forget to taste, touch, smell, hear, or see what we come upon. Language can remove us from the moment.

Walking with my toddler granddaughters was enlightening. Of course, traveling any distance took forever. We moved inch by inch. We'd take two steps and one would pick up a pebble. Roll it around. Try putting it in her mouth. I'd say, "No!" She'd toss it. Watch it bounce. After two more steps, they would explore the cracked sidewalk. And here is the real kicker, no matter how many times we walked that same stretch they'd find more to explore. Admittedly, this doesn't work if we are on our way to an appointment. But watching them left me wondering—*When did my world become a static backdrop for my life?*

Realizing how quickly we employ labels is more important than keeping a red pepper out of your dishwasher. We begin to confuse labeling with knowing. That leads us to believe that there *is* nothing more to discover—nothing more to encounter. It's most pernicious in our relationships with others. We look at loved ones and don't notice the subtle changes that wash over their faces in a conversation. We glance in the mirror without really seeing ourselves. We miss so much of life by sorting our experience without savoring it. If we ever realized the impact of this, we'd be overcome with grief.

What we often see are stored images. We look at others to confirm what we already know. Rarely do we see our unfolding self as we look into the mirror. We don't pause and ask: "Who is that woman staring back? Where is she going?" We know who we are. What's the point of really looking?

Disconnected from direct experience, food leaves us hungry, lovemaking is empty, and work becomes trite. Loved ones are not interesting, only predictable. The world becomes tidy, flat, and dull.

It loses what my three-year-old granddaughters showed me—life is a pebble to explore. To be fully alive is to be curious. When we leave the door of wonder ajar, life continues to enter. Spirit slides in and shows us that there is more to embrace.

It's a cool, sunny San Francisco morning. I'm sitting outside at Toast, a trendy café perched at the corner of Church and Day streets. It's my usual stop on my walk to the painting workshop. Pearl-black pigeons with emerald and magenta neck feathers coo as their heads bob toward the sidewalk. Green tea steams in my cup. Women with chattering children inch down the sidewalk. Busy people rush along. Everyone is headed somewhere. Even the debris that blows past appears to know where it's going.

What would it be like to live here? I wonder.

Then I see her. Put together. Hair just so. Blackberry. Briefcase. Each stride up hilly Church Street says, "I mean business." As she passes, another side of her appears. Twelve inky inches of green vines and red roses adorn her left calf. Her tattooed leg sends a message from her soul: *There is more to me than these stylish clothes—more under the surface.*

That leg says: *Sometimes, maybe not today, but some days—I run wild. I gallop. Given the right moment, I'll toss this chic black coat. I'll ditch my meeting. Peel off these layers—and maybe I'll run naked until I plunge into brisk San Francisco Bay. But for now, I'm on my way to the land of Blackberries and briefcases.*

That rose-tattooed woman is a modern mermaid—a mystery wrapped in Donna Karan cashmere. Like her, we also live in two worlds. For us the division is between a quick intellect and slower sensuous knowing. Our brain, with its lightning speed, forms conclusions and theories before what we are sensing is known to us. Appreciating our body's wisdom requires we slow down. Its messages take time to reach us.

Weaving concepts and senses together gives us finely textured perceptions. Until we join these two worlds, we mostly see fragments—lumps of labels. Taking the time to notice the touch and taste of our experience makes life juicy. Writer and painter Henry Miller knew what happens when we take in the whole world. "The moment one gives close attention to anything, even a blade of grass, it becomes a mysterious, awesome, indescribably magnificent world in itself." We all long for a life that is crisp and vivid.

A prediction about what's happening or what will take place next helps us survive. It can also obscure the subtleties of awareness. To be present is an art. It takes slowing down. What is it I see, hear, feel, smell, and taste in this moment? Engaging in that inquiry drops us into the here and now. Red peppers are confused for coffee mugs when we fail to make a distinction between our direct experience and a concept. But moments spiced by sensory input are vibrant—they remain—we remember them. First we have to notice what's right in front of us.

⁓

Back home in Chicago, it's the coldest morning in seven months. I'm soaking in a tubful of lavender and Epsom salts. Today is set aside for writing and painting. But before the keys will click or the paint will fly, the "soft animal of my body" needs attention. That Mary Oliver phrase from "Wild Geese" reminds me to listen to my body. And on this day, it longs to be immersed in silky warm water. I slide deeper into a claw-foot tub, hoping the cold, hungry winds won't find me.

Immersed in liquid warmth I appreciate the two worlds that live in me. One part longs to race ahead, to sort life into predictable patterns—longs to be in charge. The other part wishes to sink in and inhabit the moment, explore the mystery. One part creates concepts and forms plans. The other relies on body wisdom gained by spontaneous sensory experiences. Labeling is necessary. But it freezes life into images and lets us believe we have mastery over the mystery.

What would happen if my labeled world thawed? Maybe then I'd see labels as tools. But for now they frequently dominate my experience. They cut off what I see before I fully engage with what is before me. Outside the window, my garden is losing its battle to freezing winds. Elephant-eared hostas collapse on the ground like flimsy paper. They are no match for a wintry frost. Earth has begun to pull them into her underground belly.

Looking at them I think, *Even though I know your name, in Latin and in English, I don't really know you. Even though I planted you—you do not belong to me. You belong to the earth. You belong to some mystery my eyes cannot see—my words cannot name. You are not mine. I am not mine. I belong to a mystery that holds me, feeds me, and breathes me.*

Later, I will take my blue mug, filled with hot coffee, and carry it downstairs to my studio. Paint will begin to cover crisp white sheets of paper. For a short time, I'll forget I know the names of things. I'll cross some mysterious threshold that is always available. Nudged by the aroma of morning coffee or even the sound of a passing car, the land of labels falls away. This new land waits for us at the tip of our senses. There the ordinary becomes extraordinary.

Where is the entrance?

It's wherever *we* are.

We can even enter through a red pepper.

Bees

Savoring the Senses

How we spend our days is, of course, how we spend our lives.
Annie Dillard

I am a beached mermaid, swept out of the flow of my life.
Only I'm not at sea but in my kitchen with the TV remote
in my hand. My finger pauses above the "on" button. Distraction. If I press it, I won't notice how bored I feel. Stuck. Lodged
between the same three things I fix for breakfast every morning
and the memory of more vibrant moments.

For years, I raced out of the house after packing lunches and sending kissed husband and children on their way. On busy mornings, it
was easier to let *moments* race past. Then I lived in a future created
by my plans for the day. Now that I work from home most days, it's
obvious that moments come and go and—I'm just not there.

Sometimes, just the recognition of how disconnected we feel can bring us back to the moment. It does that for me. I put down the remote, spot a tomato on the counter; gather basil, onions, olive oil, salt, pepper, and my sharp knife. Chop. Chop. Chop. Voila! A quick salsa emerges. I combine it with a scrambled egg and wrap it in a warm tortilla. The spicy and fresh concoction is delicious. My taste buds applaud.

The tang of coffee washes over my tongue as the room comes into focus. Spikes of Russian Sage burst out of a nearby vase. Flowers bring life to a room, especially if they are from your own garden. Yesterday they grew in a misty-blue clump near the maple tree. Irresistible. I'd cut each stem as bees arrived and departed like planes at the world's busiest airport. Bees love blue flowers.

Why do bees prefer blue flowers? I wonder. That would make a great Google search. It might even make a good Jeopardy question. The quality that attracts bees to blue … The question Alex, What is…? I could research that.

The delight of tortilla and flowers fade. My head's abuzz. Mentally, I begin a Google search. *Bees. Blue Flowers. Nectar.* I love researching topics. At times, they are essential to my work. On this morning, it was a ploy to avoid my disquiet. When I feel uneasy, I often look for some form of a dancing monkey to distract me. It is always a critical juncture. One I know so well—the crossroads between diversion and engagement. The choice is busywork or sinking into the moment—no matter what I might be experiencing. Journaling, writing, painting, or meditating would help me engage the restlessness.

Recently, I attended a nature writing class. The instructor's guidelines reminded me that to stay aware of the present moment is a practice. This morning my focus flits from one thing to another. The writing teacher's instructions are helpful: "observe, feel without judging, and follow your senses." Doing this allows us to drop into the moment. The poet Allen Ginsberg called this "noticing what you notice."

One of the nature-writing students asked a great question:

"With so much to look at in any setting, where do we put our attention?" Without skipping a beat the teacher said, "Wherever it will take you deeper." In any moment, we can engage or stay on the surface. If we are standing in a field of flowers or in our kitchen, it's the same question. What will take me deeper? What will bring me present? Turning on the TV this morning or doing that Google search would have been a detour.

But what keeps us from staying in the present moment?

Days later I was still wondering about this question.

Washing my teapot and putting it away I thought, *Habitual actions make us numb.* I slipped the pot into its place on the shelf and remembered the Japanese tea ceremony. It's an elaborate ritual centered on the making and serving of tea. But what is the difference between a ritual and a habit? Both are repeated actions. Then I saw it. Rituals, like the tea ceremony, saying a mantra, or the Rosary, call for focused awareness. That is the difference. Rituals have an underlying intention of consciousness.

In truth, I could have prepared any of my old breakfast choices and been present. It isn't *what* we are doing that brings us present. Making tea is just making tea unless we do it intentionally. It isn't the "what" but the "how" that makes the difference. Focused awareness turns rote actions into spirited activities. My morning shifted when I observed my situation. Noticing is often the first step to reaching deeper moments of appreciation.

But why care about what takes us "deeper"?

As Joseph Campbell said in an interview with Bill Moyers, "We're seeking an experience of being alive...so that we actually feel the rapture of being alive." Paying attention brings us into that rapture. It's possible to move through life without feeling the delight of being alive. Like the water-skimming bugs on the creek near my childhood home, it is possible to live without getting wet.

What sounds do you hear? Voices outside the room? Cars on the street? Do you feel the pressure of your body on the cushion or chair that holds you? Frequently this is how the groups I facilitate begin. We close our eyes and silently check in with all five senses. Like fine threads, the senses weave our experience of now. They help us connect to our core and speak from there. We have to touch, taste, smell, hear, and see our way to our voice. It rides deeper in our experience than buzzing thoughts.

"So much of our life passes in a comfortable blur. Living in the senses requires an easily triggered sense of marvel, a little extra energy, and most people are lazy about life. Life is something that happens to them while they wait for death." Diane Ackerman's observation in a *Natural History of the Senses* makes me wince. It's harsh. But when I look at how I spend my time, I agree. I avoid shifting my awareness to my senses. Instead, I reach for food, entertainment, or the next thing on my to-do list.

There are many explanations of why it's difficult to live in the now. Usually we say it's because we're too busy. Overloaded schedules, our modern dilemma, won't allow it. At least we think it's unique to this era. Listen to this warning: "Beware of the barrenness in a busy life." It sounds like a headline from Oprah's *O* magazine. "Is all that busyness leaving you feeling empty?" This admonition is ancient. Being present is a challenge that has been with us for centuries.

"Beware of the barrenness in a busy life," Socrates cautioned 2,500 years ago. We might question the time demands placed on ancient people. It seems funny to consider that they could even know how frantic life can be. But outside conditions are not the main problem. Truthfully, we can always find distractions, even on a vacation or a retreat, or during a soothing massage.

Socrates is telling us it's a mistake to think activity equals a full life. Busyness is just busyness unless we're acting with purpose. Racing aimlessly leaves us feeling empty and depleted. Slowing down and being attentive for even a few minutes each day will enhance our lives. It is a proven healing balm for stressed nerves. Comedian Lily Tomlin has the formula to mend a chaotic life: "For fast-acting relief, try slowing down." But slowing down is becoming a lost art. We avoid it. Why? Quiet reflection exposes knotty questions we don't want to hear.

Under all this scurrying, is the question: Who am I when I'm not busy?

Crinkly lines around Don's blue eyes smooth out. My shoulders drop, as taut muscles begin to release. Ouray, Colorado is our unwinding place. We've been here many times over the last ten years. The San Juan Mountains are huge arms that welcome us. We say we are home, even though we don't live here. From the moment the twenty-seat plane lands in Montrose, we start to relax. The tightness in my voice begins to loosen. This letting go is especially noticeable as we drive through the primeval forest between Ouray and Telluride.

Our second-hand Jeep Cherokee pulls off Highway 62. The tires that hummed on blacktop now crackle and pop on the loose gravel of Last Dollar Road, a Colorado backcountry byway. Mountain streams trickle over the road. Water sparkles as it gouges the rusty dirt under our wheels. Don silently guides the Jeep around potholes and the occasional fallen branch. I watch and listen.

Chalky aspen trees are vibrant against a pine and spruce backdrop. Their white trunks are too plentiful to count. But am I really seeing lots of trees? Aspens shoot up from a single root system that stretches over large amounts of land. In fact, the Pando aspen stand in Utah covers 106 acres. It's called the largest organism in the world. What looks like many is one.

My link to Don and everything around us is now like that of the aspen's roots: invisible. We've slipped into another world with unseen bonds. We feel them. Nothing seems separate. We stay silent. Words might break this spell. This connectedness is what I lose rushing through my days. Speed lets me forget the root system I share with nature, other people, and my own soul. Inching along this bumpy road, we are enfolded in a living web.

The road dips, turns, and opens onto high alpine meadows and sprawling ranches. Cows and horses meander unaware of our presence. Wildflowers dot the tawny grasses in pink, blue, and yellow. Their names are as charming as their appearance: Indian paintbrush, blue bells, alpine sunflowers. Near trail's end, the road drops down into the red rock cliffs of the San Miguel River basin. When we turn left onto route 145 toward Telluride, the sun reappears along with our chatter and other cars. But the silence of the forest and how I felt there stays with me.

The unity we discover in a forest is the experience of *being present*. We long for the harmony found there. It relaxes us. It awakens us. Of course, there is a practical side to living in the moment. It keeps us from missing our exit as we sail down the highway. But its greatest gift is the reminder of who we are at our core. In nature's silence we can discover what Coleman Barks, translator of the poet Rumi, says: "I think we all have a core that's ecstatic, that knows and that looks up in wonder." Who hasn't marveled at what they experience; looking up at a mountain, across the ocean, or into the velvety folds of a rose?

Life can be this way when "we notice what we notice."

Brushed on the scrolls that hang in Japanese tea rooms, "Ichi-go ichi-e" is at the heart of the tea ceremony. It's translated as "one time, one meeting," reminding those taking tea that this instant will never come again. Each second is a treasure. Every gathering is a once in a lifetime event. It isn't always possible to immerse ourselves in nature. But even a cup of tea can return us to the fullness in each moment.

Bees are wise. They size up how much energy it will take to collect nectar from a particular flower. The extraction process creates a dramatic drop in their body's temperature. They choose carefully. Blue flowers have deeper colored petals that act like little solar panels. The sweet fluid bees seek simmers like hot cocoa in dark colored flowers. Shivering cold drinks found in pale plants are not as attractive. A drink from them is like downing ice tea on a freezing day. It depletes body heat. Clever bees go for warm liquids found in indigo and sapphire blooms.

That morning in my kitchen, I was trying to decide where to land. Restlessness was telling me, *Slip down inside of your experience. Turn off the cable news, look under your uneasiness.* Like the nature-writing teacher said: "Observe, feel without judging, and follow your senses." What we see, smell, touch, taste, and hear enriches us. It reminds us of our connection to an invisible world. Some discover this through music. For others it's a craft or an art form that enraptures. Still others find that nature leaves them astonished and in a timeless state. Life holds this promise for all of us—if we pay attention.

Such moments return us to essence. Like the bee's blue flowers, they help us maintain inner warmth. Choosing well is important. Some activities deplete our energy and others fill us. Our recognition of the difference is critical. What would our days be like if we crawled into more honeyed moments of now? How can we drop into the pollen of the senses and let them cover us like fairy dust?

When I feel like a beached mermaid, it's because I've become busy rather than engaged. I've tried to swim around something rather than sink into it. Boredom and restlessness are reminders. They appear when it's time to "notice what we notice." The voice that waits to unfold reverberates with wonder. Drenched in the present, it can call for action or silence. It contains our emotions as well as what we sense. That voice vibrates with passion for life, and the spontaneous undigested experience of now.

It's the voice of our soul.

Bananas

Tending the Spark

All the arts we practice are apprenticeship. The big art is our life.
M. C. Richards

ermaids are everywhere in Mexico. Margarita-sipping mermaids adorn cafés. Their reclining bodies decorate taco trucks. Street vendors sell lottery tickets with these topless temptresses proudly displayed. They are often depicted as chubby. I find that pleasing. One aquatic babe is depicted as an unlikely passenger on the back of bicycle, her long tail swung to one side as she clutches the peddling man. Mythological creatures are at home in colorful Mexico.

It's a perfect place to offer a process painting workshop! I have found an ideal site. The Quinta Quetzalcoatl (QQ) Inn welcomes guests to the home where D. H. Lawrence lived when he wrote the first draft of *The Plumed Serpent*. It's an environment that evokes creativity. Mossy niches with benches, ponds, and fountains dot the grounds. Gargoyle and goddess statues guard vine-covered stairways. Casitas encircle a lush tropical garden. We set up our studio among the banana plants, rosebushes, and frangipani.

Paintings like prayer flags stretch around the *palapa*. Its thatched roof and open sides let the Mexican sun in and shield us from any unlikely rain. Six women dot the perimeter of the structure while another half dozen stand painting in its center. Turtles from a nearby pond creep by as we work. The scent of bougainvillea rides on warm breezes. Babbling spotted wrens serenade us. Outside pressures and demands fall away. Our bodies begin to soften.

The genius of the painting process, created by Michele Cassou, is the lack of comments or critiques about the paintings. Teachers and students put their attention on the journey, not an end product. We reclaim our authenticity through focus on the process rather than the outcome. We move through obstacles that have stopped us in the past. Intuition strengthens. Blocked places open.

Self-doubt is often the first obstacle we face. This is a human dilemma. We don't need to be painters to encounter waning confidence. Step outside the usual way of doing almost anything and you'll meet unending cautions: *Stop! You don't know how to do that. Stop! You look foolish. Stop! What will they think of you?* Admonitions like this drain enthusiasm. If we heed these warnings, we struggle to keep moving. Eventually, we'll stop. Intuition's gentle nudges are lost.

The painting process is a metaphor for living in the moment. It teaches us to trust whatever appears without knowing what comes next. Images spring from the tips of brushes. Delight and surprise wash over the students' faces. Their eyes fill with tears. Still they paint. One woman squats as she works. Red tempera, like the blood of new life, runs off the edge of her paper. Her work is raw and alive. We gathered here to explore spontaneous expression, not to become better painters.

It's liberating!

Scientists researching spontaneous expression made a fascinating discovery. They gave chimpanzees paint, paper, and brushes. The chimps began painting like young children. Slashes of bright colors filled one sheet after the other. Then the researchers gave them a banana after each painting. Their enthusiasm dwindled with each payoff. After a short time they made one swipe of color on a sheet and waited for their reward.

Joy vanished.

They were seduced by the prize. How clear this seems. When actions are ignited by an inner fire we become lost in the moment. Time stands still. Authentic expression becomes its own reward. Shift your motivation to an external reward and the inner fire cools. Passion and self-discovery die out. How this misdirected focus must impact our children! How must it impact *us*? Acting to receive rewards obscures an important truth. A whole truckload of bananas will never equal the joy of expressing our inner spark.

Even though we may envy people with piles of these tropical delights, some place in us realizes it isn't about the banana. What we long for is genuine self-expression. Not everything that we say or do can come from this place. Sometimes we need to earn bananas in order to eat. But a life focused on payoffs needs to be balanced with playful curiosity. Play is a healing balm for our tired soul.

I've worked with painting students as young as five years old and discovered the same troubling dynamic. They have already learned to seek approval as their incentive to act. For some this becomes a lifelong pattern. Others grow tired of this outer focus and recognize a hunger for something else.

That is when the painstaking work of freeing oneself begins. Theologian Matthew Fox said it this way: "every liberation movement is about the release of the artist within people, that part of us that expresses our deepest self." It is clear to me that this is the work of becoming an adult. Growing down into ourselves is finding, trusting, and protecting our deepest self.

⁂

Four years old, I lean into the carved edges of my mother's hope chest. It's just the right size to be my desk. While she's cleaning her closet, I have paper and crayons to keep me busy. Her irresistible lipstick sits on the dressing table. Now I hold this shiny tube in my hand—not for my lips but for my paper. Revlon Red glides across snow-white sheets. It's so much more fun than crayons.

My mother turns around. Surprisingly, she is smiling with a look that says I am her cute and clever child. "Look, you made a lamb," she says. I didn't know what it was. It was the result of circular motions that I loved making. She steps back into the closet and returns to her task. Now I want to see her smile. My paper fills with smears of red as I move the tube from side to side. That will really make her happy. Very little white remains on my paper when she turns around. Expectantly I hold my paper up for her approval but it is disappointment, not delight in her eyes. "You've ruined it. I can't see the lamb." I let go of the thrill of making circles in the hope of pleasing her. Now I had neither.

These moments, tucked in our memories, are often forgotten. They return at the thought of picking up a brush or pencil. Or we feel a curious uneasiness at the suggestion of trying anything "creative." Fear rears its toothy head. We retreat. Often these early interactions are not deliberately hurtful. My mother was encouraging, and yet she unintentionally intruded into my exploration. The desire for praise makes it easy to abandon self-satisfaction. Desire for approval is the genesis of the false self, a self that moves strategically in order to garner favor.

External focus gives the doubting voice room to wiggle into our awareness. Soon it is using a megaphone to grab our attention. When it happens, we stop searching for an inner connection and scan our environment for what we "should" do. Our intuitive voice is muffled. It's replaced by a voice with a litany of demands. According to Pam Grout, author of *Living Big*, this is the "same voice that tells you you're expendable, the voice that assigns you a number, a punch card, a place in line... It's the voice desperately afraid that you're going to figure it out."

And what is the "it" that we might figure out?

It's that we have an inner spark waiting for expression.

A creative force runs through us. It isn't available to just a small number of artistic folks.

It is available to everyone. Whether we are producing software, designing a car or creating a piece of music, we touch that same waiting mystery. It greets us when we're willing to risk mistakes and are flexible about the outcome. The question isn't, "Am I creative?" The question is, "Do I recognize it?" "Do I nurture it?"

Self-estrangement occurs when we don't tend our inner spark. For some of us it means ensuring that we have enough time to write, paint, or garden. For others it is belly-dancing, backpacking, or being with friends. Enthusiasm nurtures this spark. Where we find it differs. What we need are activities that are their own reward: soul-satisfying acts, like the childlike joy of watching clouds.

Lama Govinda warns us of the outcome of ignoring this need in *Way of White Clouds*: "When every detail of our life is planned and regulated, and every fraction of time determined beforehand, then the last trace of our boundless and timeless being, in which the freedom of our soul exists, will be suffocated."

It's important to recognize when our flame is dwindling. My signals are obvious to my husband. I get grumpy. Everything becomes deadly serious. I'm not fun to be with. No one can please me. This often happens gradually, and that makes it hard to recognize. I don't want to be with anyone and no one wants to be with me.

It feels awful when I've given up on myself. No one but me can fix it. When I look back, it's clear that I stopped paying attention to the things that sustain me. The breeze of a busy life blew out my flame. Or I've let my critic stop me. To be loyal to our own being is at the heart of finding our voice. This realization calls for hard choices about how we spend our time and money. Ultimately, we have to take a stand for what we cherish.

It takes courage.

As students left, I imagined them crisscrossed with new neural pathways leading from their brushes to their hearts. Each time we express our inner fire we create a clearer return route. We left the QQ Inn with paint under our fingernails and an experience of spontaneous expression. The process and the environment worked together to remind us of our longing for unfettered play. Okay, of course there will be more blocks. Energy will drain. We'll get lost. Connecting to our core takes an incredible amount of perseverance no matter which road we take.

Bodacious Mexican mermaids remind me that spontaneity is an essential ingredient in a satisfying life. It's a vital addition to being productive. These mischievous maidens carry me back to the joy of watching Revlon Red circles appear across snowy sheets of paper. They're a reminder that life is *not* about the bananas. Maybe these

fishy ladies won't always be my soul's guides, but for now finding them anywhere delights me. My response to them is always the same. I smile.

When I read a Mary Oliver poem, look at the lines in a Frank Gehry building, or marvel at Georgia O'Keefe's gigantic flowers, I experience their distinctive individual energy. But it's awash in something bigger. I recognize it. I sense the same place in me. It's in all of us. Unknowable, yet available. We each have a spark of consciousness to express. The form it takes is not important. Poet Pablo Neruda said, "All paths lead to the same goal: to convey to others and ourselves what we are."

We are alive for one reason: to give voice to that spark.

Hag

Embracing What's Real

Age has given me what I was looking for my entire life. It gave me—me.
Anne Lamott

My eyes peer through two shriveled slits as the latex mask slips over my head. I am becoming Baba Yaga, the hag of folklore and fairytale fame. A stringy wig slides into place to cover my hair. Securing it, I tie on a brightly flowered babushka. Nails I often polish are left unpainted. I step into the yard and scratch my fingers across bare ground. Earth filled fingernails along with wrinkle-laden, mismatched layers of clothing nearly finish the guise.

Not quite.

I place a basket, filled with potentially perilous apples, over my arm. The transformation is now complete. I no longer look my age of forty-four. I appear as a wily ninety-four. *Perfect*, I say to myself. *This is who I'll be for Halloween. Not a playful witch, but a scary, snaggle-toothed, craggy creature.*

Initially, I was only going to greet trick-or-treaters at home. I left my therapy office early to make the change from compassionate listener to cunning old crone. It takes less effort to embody her than I imagined. My unsuspecting visitors will not arrive for a while. But I can't wait. I walk a couple of blocks to our local library and startle a few librarians. They're friends and acquaintances, but most don't recognize me. I never break character or speak—at least not in my own voice.

I cackle.

Neighbors encountered on my way back home pull their children in close and refuse to take the candy I offer. My true identity as friendly neighbor is skillfully buried. Drunk with the power to repulse, I drive to my husband's office. The looks from his co-workers delight me. Brawny men recoil nervously. They understand that the wise approach a dangerous old woman with trepidation—or not at all.

Playing the hag in all her awfulness delights me. This unsightly character is free from the princess' need for perfection. The hag may not be the one we invite to work, to pour tea, or to comfort a baby. Still, she has a place. Her ferocious energy can go toe-to-toe with bullies. She is fearless. She writes, paints, and dances with abandon. The critic doesn't sway her. The hag cares not how others judge her. Her repulsiveness releases her from the jail of perfection. It frees her from seeking approval.

When a woman becomes interested in exploring the hag, she is ready to grow down into herself. The hag's unattractive energy resides under the mask of the princess. Playing in this rarely visited inner region awakens the power to love our warts. Few women want to see themselves as a hag. Most long to make peace with discordant emotions or "flaws." To strengthen the connection to our voice we must welcome and embrace all of us…the pretty and the profane. Coming home to ourselves in this way is the best kind of homecoming. Warts are then seen as part of what makes us a loveable mess.

Poet Laureate William Stafford was asked about his daily practice of writing a poem. The questioner wondered what he did on the days his poem didn't measure up. His reply is revealing and liberating. He said, "I lower my standards."

Growing up is something that's expected of us. Growing down into who we are calls for compassion. We don't receive instructions on how to do this. However, Stafford's response is a great clue. He didn't say *give up*. He didn't say *throw away* any imperfect poems. He said *accept where you are*. Growing down into ourselves takes radical acceptance.

Ironically, Pulitzer Prize winner Mary Schmich of the Chicago Tribune wrote an article on the princess or witch costume choice about the same time I was scaring burly men and stunned librarians. Schmich writes that after encountering girls repeatedly choosing the princess side of the equation she wants to cry, "Ditch the princess regalia, girls! …. Don't be afraid to show your inner witch." I share her enthusiasm for the hag in a culture that's obsessed with the princess.

Matching tiaras and tutus don't concern the hag. She's interested in what is on the inside more than the outside. There is a time to play the princess. When we are young women, we explore the currency of our looks. It is a time of glitter and sparkle. Princesses experience power by attracting the Prince's attention. The hag's power comes from finding it deep within her own core.

Fairy tales frequently feature both a princess and a hag. Predictably they encounter one another. Once they meet, the young sweet one will fall into a deep sleep, disappear into the woods, or die. It's inevitable. The princess cannot imagine anyone causing her harm. Without this awareness she places herself at great risk. When peril appears, she will dismiss it. She will *always* eat the poisoned apple. It shimmers, therefore it must be safe.

What makes the hag so terrifying? She will not avert her gaze from death, decay, or danger. Exploring them intrigues her. She's not afraid to look you straight in the eye. When she does, it feels as if she sees into your soul. There is nowhere and nothing to hide in her presence. Searching not only your eyes but also her own heart, she discovers life's deepest truths. Spending time alone helps the hag maintain this inner focus. The princess, on the other hand, avoids solitude. For her, being alone means bumping into what she cannot accept about herself.

In the story of the Little Mermaid, the hag is a sea witch. She provides magic, giving the mermaid legs, a chance for love, and a shot at a human soul. Let's just say asking a hag for help is often a dicey thing and always has a cost. For the Little Mermaid it meant the loss of her beautiful voice. Contact with the hag often means the demise of naiveté. To be naïve is to know but not heed what we know. The hag is an illusion breaker. Once we encounter her, risk-free living is seen for what it is—a fantasy. Her arrival ushers in wisdom and wonder.

Predictably, exterior beauty fades. If we value attractiveness above all else, we'll fail to discover the hag's strength. Each time we silence her, our own wise voice weakens. Clarissa Pinkola Estes writes in *The Dangerous Old Woman* that the secret to keeping and renewing our spirit is "to be old while young, and young while old." In our youth the practice is to listen to our elders, including our own inner wise self. As we age, the challenge is to allow the counsel of our young hearts to keep innocence and wonder alive.

My Great-Grandmother Dory had very red hair. As my mother said, "She helped it along with henna." Even as a child I had doubts about the color. It was Bozo-esque. Henna turned her hair bright orange. That is what happens when it's applied to white hair. Carrot-colored hair next to her milky Norwegian skin intensified the effect. But that is where the clown comparison ended. Grandma Dory was a no-nonsense woman.

Paper-thin skin covered my grandmother's hands. Blue veins crisscrossed bony branches connected to her knuckles. Coffee-colored spots were sprinkled here and there. Poking and pleating the skin on the back of her hands, I'd watch as it ever so slowly smoothed out. Normally impatient, she endured my innocent curiosity. She washed my face and tucked me into bed with the same hands that once helped her wriggle into a roll of carpet when at sixteen she became a stowaway. She hid until the ship leaving Norway for New York was securely at sea.

Now in my sixties, I am a grandmother myself. Each of my granddaughters in their chubby, cute years has explored my changing face. They'd wiggle loose skin under my chin. Caution me about my teeth yellowing. Question me about sparse eyelashes, identify renegade hairs on my face. Reese, our youngest, gasped in horror when she spotted red lines running through my eyeballs.

I am a woman of wrinkles and misplaced hairs.

I am also *their* future.

Champa incense burns in a brass dish by the front door. My house feels and smells like an ashram where mornings are quiet and meditative. For a decade I spent days and sometimes weeks in ashrams learning the value of inner quiet. Stays there made it easy to slip into stillness. Now in the early mornings I work to create that same feeling. It lets me notice things I often miss. Snowflakes fall in slow motion outside my window as I sit watching them. In a world that is forever speeding up—talking faster, moving faster, and making quick decisions—falling snow belongs to another world. That world isn't concerned with hurrying.

This is my process of restoration:

I turn off the phone, I ignore email. I paint. I write or sit in silence. Pondering is possible in peacefulness... *What does it mean to have a voice ... a woman's voice?* I wonder. I know that a woman who has not found this inner still place is at the mercy of her soundings. Tossed from one demand for help to another, she will not discover her core. That requires time alone.

Hydrangeas that were once extravagant with blooms have been cut back. Their stubby stems poke out of icy patches of earth. Sky is the grey of a confederate soldier's uniform. Everything visible is a shadow of its summer self. It all looks dead. Yet spring has already begun. Deep under the frozen surface, plants send slender shoots in all directions.

Growth often begins out of sight.

Mammals who wear clothes, drive cars and worry about the future—that's who we humans are. Our animal selves react quickly to what we see. These reactions often occur before we make a considered response. Yesterday I walked through a stand of pine trees.

Longing to carry the peace found there home with me, I reached down and picked up a pinecone. The first one I saw was scruffy. Many of its seeds were missing. As I slipped it into my pocket I saw one with every seed in place. Now I wanted the perfect one.

The perfectionist in us prefers a flawless specimen. Yet there is another way. The gap between thought and action is the act of being mindful. That pause returns us to the moment. We start to see past the surface of what we encounter. Ordinary changes that occur over time reveal their beauty when we linger.

Wabi-Sabi is Japanese for a way of living that emphasizes finding beauty in imperfection and embracing natural cycles of growth and decay. In this practice we learn to appreciate spring's bare branches and winter's frozen plants. We experience the beauty in the beginning or the decline of things. A chipped pot shows its loving use. Use gives the pot character. Frayed fabric on a chair where a loved one sat to read helps us remember them. And as author May Sarton warns, "A house that does not have one worn, comfy chair in it is soulless." Wabi-Sabi asks us to see subtle elegance in scruffy pinecones. It points out that imperfections let the soul shine through things—through us. It teaches that "nothing is perfect, nothing lasts, and nothing is finished."

Wabi-Sabi celebrates cracks in pottery and even lines on faces. It embraces crevices in leather or wrinkles on knees. It says marks that happen over time add to the preciousness of things. Could this include liver spots? It is the practice of finding charm in flaws that occur in the loving use of anything. Can we extend this awareness so that we embrace our changing bodies?

My quest *is* to appreciate my own aging body. Some days that is easier than others. The old latex mask is gone. I know the crone personally now. She peeks at me when I look in the mirror. The princess is still whispering and occasionally shouts her demands for a light-filled life. Yet it is evermore clear that it takes silence and darkness to discover what is real. So I avoid listening to her and seek solitude. Solitude calls with increasing urgency as we age.

It is essential.

Stillness sharpens our sense of meaning and value. It strengthens our reliance on inner guidance. That connection is critical in a culture that continues to tout a focus on surface beauty. I am leaving flowers in vases longer these days and watching the changes that occur. Ruby roses display deeper colors of red as they curl up and dry out. The delicacy of dying daffodils pleases me as their petals turn tissue-thin. Looking at them reminds me of my great-grandmother Dory's fragile skin. Not throwing out flowers at the first sign of fading lets me appreciate the changes that all living things traverse.

The "warts and all" way of life frees us. It takes practice—lots of practice, a sense of humor and patience. When Anne Lamott says "age . . . gave me—me," I think that if pressed, she'd say, Finding one's self is a gift of aging. But it is a gift that takes work to unwrap. Old patterns are stubborn. Mindfulness provides the pause that interrupts habitual reactions. It runs counter to our quick animal nature. Courage to try this new slower way of responding is rewarded. Interrupting our reflexive reach for flawlessness we discover—the gift of great value—our true voice.

What is perfect, anyway?

Plastic houseplants appear perfect. Well, that was until manufacturers realized that to make them look real they needed to add slight imperfections. Plastic plant producers learned something we all must discover...

Perfect isn't real.

It doesn't even look real.

Tootsie Pop

Reaching Our Core

If you lived in your heart you'd be home by now.
Bumper sticker spotted on a passing car

f we meet in a doctor's waiting room, we probably won't speak to each other. Arriving with one concern or another, we won't let it show. Even if we are there for something as simple as an ingrown toenail, it's our secret. Our social antenna turned to low, we just pass time. We wait. I wish waiting rooms were more like a Starbucks with an attitude of *Come on in. We'll act like we recognize you even if we don't.* I especially prefer this approach in places where I'll soon be naked—not the coffee shop.

The receptionist delivers her line on cue. "Your doctor will be right with you." I pull out a magazine from the stack on a table as I look for a comfortable place. Identical maroon cushioned chairs with black metal frames line the perimeter of the room. I'm sure that the catalog described them to their purchaser as "comfortable cabernet cloth seats with midnight-colored steel frames." Without an inch between them, they look more like a conveyor system than a seating arrangement.

Mermaids are the furthest thing from my mind.

I'm half paying attention to a *Good Housekeeping* magazine as I wonder how much longer I'll have to sit here. On page 161, a photograph of a little girl grabs me. The title of the article, "Love without Words," intrigues me. Within the first paragraph, I discover that this engaging girl with the huge brown eyes has a brain malformation that leaves her unable to speak.

I break the first rule of a doctor's waiting room: Avoid health articles, especially if they describe a terrifying condition.

But she tugs at me.

When I look at the other photos I think, *Schuyler would fit nicely into our tribe of granddaughters. She'd shorten the gap between Lilly who's nine and Reese who's four.* Her father, Rob, is about the age of our son. His tender and irreverent words are riveting. His devotion pulsates through each paragraph. He calls the condition "Schuyler's Monster." And when I turn to the second page of the article, I see it. There, floating above a column of words is a heading in bold red print—"Mermaid."

I had to read more.

Schuyler, like most little girls, loves mermaids. But she shares a unique bond with them. A connection she discovered while watching Disney's *Little Mermaid*. In that story the heroine, Ariel, loses her voice. For the first time, Schuyler communicated to her parents through the aide of an electronic device, *I can't talk.* Although it's true she cannot speak, Schuyler does connect with others: she reaches them through her exuberance. This story left me wondering about the message in the article's title: Love Without Words. Can voice also be beyond words? I turn to my old friend Google for help. But it fails me. It is frustrating. People refer to voice without saying what they mean, even when they describe how to find it.

Stephen Covey, the business guru, said that voice is the pathway to greatness. "Voice is the overlapping of the four parts of our nature: our body, our mind, our heart, and our spirit." He has an elaborate plan of how to find your voice. Maybe I'm trying to catch light in a bottle, but I want a definition and can't find one in his book. Parts are inspirational and informative, but what he explains sounds more like a location and outcome than a definition.

Playwright and actor Sam Shepard said in an interview that voice exists in the spaces between words. Strangely, this rings true to me. It points to voice as phenomenon. Covey said where it is. Shepard says where it isn't. I'm starting to see just how slippery voice is.

Carol Gilligan's groundbreaking book, *In a Different Voice,* explored how women express who they are. And though voice had a prominent place in the title and appeared throughout the book, she didn't define it. Eleven years later in a second edition, she struggled to clarify it. When I read her words, these phrases jumped out at me. *Voice is a channel connecting inner and outer worlds…*voice is…*the core of the self.*

Martha Graham, the famous performer and choreographer, explained self-expression this way: "There is a vitality, a life force, a quickening that is translated through your actions, and because there is only one of you in all time, this expression is unique. If you block it, it will never exist through any other medium. It will be lost… Keep the channel open." Here is that word *channel* again.

What is it that waves through the channel from core to outer world?

When questions become this lofty, it helps to bring them down to earth. Liz Carpenter, the social secretary to Lady Bird Johnson and speechwriter for LBJ, wrote a book about her experience in the White House. Later she appeared on a panel theorizing about what it takes to become an author. Hemingway, Lord Byron, and Tolstoy quotes scattered the comments of other participants. The air was thin and the useful advice thinner. As Joseph Epstein recalls in *A Line Out For a Walk*, then Liz spoke: "I'll tell you what—you want to be a writer, honey, find a comfortable chair."

In honor of Liz Carpenter's no nonsense approach, I offer the "Tootsie Pop Theory of Personality Development." This theory explains the difficulty we encounter discovering our voice. As we mature, outer layers cover our core self, be they cherry, orange, or grape. They protectively crystallize around our soft vulnerable center. We can describe the layers, report on their condition, or tell stories about how they formed. But speaking from this veneer doesn't reflect who we are. To realize our voice we must speak from our core.

Here is where the tasty analogy falls apart. Breaking through to the chewy center of a Tootsie Pop is delightful. But in life, we often reach our core after something collapses in our lives. When we crack through our own outer layers, there is agony, not delight. Our self-image crumbles. We feel naked. When we speak through that brokenness, our voice comes from a new place. *It comes from our core.*

Virginia Woolf, English novelist and essayist, sat at her large desk or stood and wrote. Her words, sent out into the world on hundreds of pages, were not embraced but rejected. At the age of forty, in the rubble of failed books, something opened up in her. In that vulnerable state, she wrote these touching words in her diary: "There is no doubt in my mind, that I have found out how to begin to say something in my own voice."

In 2008 during the New Hampshire Democratic Presidential Primary, candidate Hillary Clinton told voters, "You listened to me and I found my voice." I don't know if she actually found her voice in that emotional moment, but the events demonstrated what I know to be critical to this process. Finding our voice often occurs after a breakdown of sorts.

People questioned how Hillary Clinton, with thirty-five years of public life, could not have found her voice until then. But finding our voice is not a one-time event. It will occur repeatedly in a life. These periods of shakiness and pain are part of the discovery process. Our voice isn't given to us. It takes work. It requires that we recognize there is something of great value at our core.

Hillary said something else that is critical to the discovery of voice. She said, "You listened to me." There is a call and response process in finding our voice. As a psychotherapist and group facilitator, I've learned that listening is more important than a brilliant assessment. Listening can return speakers to themselves. In the process, we can both discover what is unspoken between the words. To speak, to be listened to and to have it reflected back is part of the unearthing. Many of us long to receive these simple sentences. I see you. I hear you. What you are saying makes a difference to me.

Listening is critical because voice is hard to discover on our own. We won't walk into a room and find it lying on a table. It isn't rolled up in our sock drawer. It is not a thing. It lives in our experience. Yet we speak about voice as if it is a thing. It isn't. It's important to remember that. A single word like *voice* can't capture everything that we mean when we say it. At best, it points to what we feel.

Voice is a phenomenon. We sense it. Even our experience of its absence tells us something. If we attempt to capture it in a fistful of letters, it glides out of our grasp. Voice waves through us from core to outer world. Our best hope of locating what we mean by voice is to trace it through our own experience. When did we speak in our true voice? When didn't we?

Doctors were more than MDs in the 1960s. They were MDeities. They had absolute power in healthcare decisions. In the middle of a huge corridor at the University of Chicago's Billings Hospital, I stood toe-to-toe with the head of cardiology. Everything was wrong about this picture, out of balance, a teeter-totter with all the weight on one end. He is six feet tall. I am a foot shorter. He is seasoned with frosty hair and piercing blue eyes. I'm a short-skirted, barely adult twenty-four-year-old with long flowing hair. He is an esteemed professional. I'm a stay-at-home mom with two toddlers.

Don, my husband, is down some other corridor, having arrived by ambulance a few days before.

"You can't send him home. This is what always happens. He gets better. They send him home and he gets worse." All I see are the doctor's pensive eyes and the blur of his white coat. He heard me. He kept Don for six weeks. It was a breakthrough for both of us. I spoke up with power and resolve and Don got the care he needed. Eventually, they discovered a treatment for his heart infection.

Not all moments of voice are dramatic. Most are simple everyday encounters in checkout lines, bus stops, or across breakfast tables. They occur when prescribed roles melt and hearts meet. Our voice comes through when we speak without concern for what others might think of us.

I had just seen Cormac McCarthy interviewed about his book, *The Road*. It details a father and son's painful path as two of the last survivors in a post-apocalyptic world.

It got me thinking.

The next person I met was the checker at Trader Joe's. He was helpful and friendly with tender eyes. "What would you do if you were the last person on earth?" I blurted out. He stopped. He abandoned his script somewhere between bagging the bananas and yogurt. Now he's a man pondering that devastating possibility. "I'd go find a lot of money and roll around in it. I don't think I'll ever have a lot of money and I wonder how that would feel. What would you do?" he asked, returning the favor. "The first thing I'd do is look for food. We all have our priorities." We laughed. Our assigned roles, thin as ice on a spring pond, thawed.

This is what I know about voice. It is the transmission of energy. Voice vibrates through a little girl's exuberance. It flows through the love of devoted parents. It rides in notes of music, paint on canvas, or between the words in a play. It's evident in a blueprint, a business plan, poem, or political campaign. Voice carries what Emerson called the "current of Universal Being."

I've read many definitions of voice. Most of them are confusing. It turns out that voice, like love, beauty, or pornography, is recognizable yet difficult to define. We feel a true voice as much as, maybe more than, hear it. It's that experience that we struggle to define. A true voice brings about a shift in the speaker and the listener. It's an experience that is difficult to explain.

It's tempting to think painters, artists, singers, or writers are the only ones with the karmic imperative to find their voice. Covey said that it's a critical element in corporate life also. The celebrated author of *Seven Habits of Highly Effective People* wrote an entire book on the eighth habit, a habit he defines as finding your voice and inspiring others. For decades he has taught that his seven habits will make us successful. Now he says that the eighth habit takes us to greatness. According to Covey, humans have a compelling need to find their voice. "There is a deep, innate, almost inexpressible yearning within each one of us to find our voice in life." Finding our voice isn't an esoteric pursuit but an essential human endeavor. Our paths will differ. But the desire lives within all of us.

———

10:30 p.m. Don and I settle in for the night. A freezing Chicago winter holds us in its grip. The sheets are cold as I scoot over to his side of the bed. We hold hands and look into each other's eyes. His hand is warm. His eyes are warmer. I feel the beating of his heart where our fingers and palms touch. Energy that I cannot see moves through his body. I know *him* through this unseen energy. It animates his resilient heart.

We drift into dreamtime together as we have for the last four decades. Gabriel Garcia Marquez reflected on his marriage of about the same duration when he said, "I know my wife so well that she is a great mystery to me." In our early years, we learned the landscape of outer layers. We mistook them for the core of each other. A mystery, which I will never fully know, holds me to Don.

Voice comes from our core. It pushes past rules or roles. And when it does, we recognize the essence of others and us. A shift in awareness occurs. Boundaries melt. We see each other in a new way. It is familiar and yet mysterious. In an instant, we see through outer layers. Willa Cather said when interviewed by the Nebraska State Journal, "Only a diamond can cut a diamond, only can a soul touch a soul." Our true voice reverberates with the sound of our soul. It allows souls to touch each other.

Remember the slogan for Tootsie Pops? "How many licks does it take to get to the center of a Tootsie Pop? Nobody knows for sure." Why is it so difficult to eat one and not break the outer candy? We long to reach the sumptuous center. This is also true in life. The urge to liberate the core is the root of all seeking. First, we encounter the outer layers. When they fall away, we discover a chewy mystery at our core.

Voice is our connection to that mystery.

Noxzema Jars

Cracking Open

Ring the bells that still can ring
Forget your perfect offering
There is a crack in everything
That's how the light gets in
Leonard Cohen, "Anthem"

*I*t's March. Reddington Beach, in Tampa, Florida, glistens with sunshine. My Midwestern body, pale as snow, longs for vitamin D. But I have something else in mind. The ocean is where one might find mermaids. Don and I stroll along the beach talking about the things that concern couples on vacation: the weather and where we'll eat. My gaze is on the seaweed, fish bones, and shells washing ashore. I never take my eyes off the ocean's edge. Fixed. Determined. Hopeful.

A legendary mermaid fell in love with a sailor on a passing ship. In the midst of a threatening storm, she changed the direction of the wind to save him. But Poseidon, king of the sea, had forbidden mermaids to interfere with the weather. He sent his wayward daughter to live near Davey Jones' Locker, never to resurface—Poseidon's form of grounding. Her tears of unrequited love wash upon the shore in the form of colorful shards of glass.

Some call the remnants of shattered containers *beach glass*. Others call them *mermaid's tears*. Cobalt blue Noxzema jars, amber beer bottles, and the aqua glass of old telephone insulators become gems after the ocean polishes away their rough edges. Some fragments will embellish jewelry. Others will travel home in sandy pockets and adorn tables and mantels. Mermaid's tears are a great metaphor for life. In them the broken and the mundane become a thing of beauty. Their deliverance from trash to something precious inspires me.

Broken hearts. Broken contracts. Broken health. Broken vows. Broken dreams. Broken families. Broken friendships. Broken homes. Broken promises. Life cracks us open. No one escapes the chance to find value in brokenness. In each of these situations something that's invisible splinters—our self-image. We are not the friend, employee, or wife we thought we were. We're not as healthy, rich, protected, effective, or loved as we once believed.

We're shaken to the core.

The Diagnostic and Statistical Manual of Mental Disorders is the text I used as a psychotherapist. It classifies symptoms. "Cracking open" is not one of the categories in the nearly 900 pages. Yet that's what many of my clients experienced. Loss of energy, appetite, or sexual desire was frequently the reason for an appointment. More than anything, they felt broken open. "I don't feel like my old self," they'd tell me.

Cracking open is a striking shift in how we sense the world and ourselves. Most of the time, our sense of self is in harmony with the outer world. But when an event like a ruptured relationship occurs, fissures of confusion spread through us. We are filled with questions. If we are not who we thought we were—who are we?

Our well-being depends on answering this question.

Fear fills us and the question seems unanswerable.

———

Eileen, a friend, recently published her book. She leans across the table as she shares her exciting news. God forbid that one scintillating syllable be lost to the clatter of Starbucks. I want to be happy for her. I am not. *Does she notice my uneasiness,* I wonder. I try to look away. I can't. Her words are tiny chisels that puncture my brittle walls. Through the cracks, I see that I'm unsure of my own direction.

I pretend my condition isn't obvious. My lifelessness is in stark contrast to Eileen's exuberance. My responses contain as much interest as I can muster, which isn't much. Her every word and gesture convinces me how much I want to be where she is. Dullness engulfs me. She doesn't seem to notice. As she talks, pieces of my arid life fall into my cup. Plop!

I can't bring myself to admit to her how desperate I feel. Somehow, it's easier to be honest with a fellow lost soul. Besides, I haven't even let myself know how unhappy I am, until now. In the presence of her genuine enthusiasm, it's hard to fool myself. Some people are boastful at times like this. She isn't. Eileen's sharing is authentic and passionate. It's irresistible.

I can't wait to leave.

"Who has not sat, afraid, before his own heart's curtain?" asks Rainer Maria Rilke in *The Duino Elegies*. To have that curtain pulled back and find uncertainty is, well, unsettling. That Starbucks encounter wasn't a big moment. It doesn't compare to our canceled wedding because of Don's first hospitalization, his repeated illnesses, my surgeries, my post-partum depression, or a close brush with bankruptcy. In the context of these other earthshaking events, this reads about 0.5 on my inner Richter Scale. But most of us have had the experience of a casual comment that caused a crack in our own self-confidence. They're especially troublesome when they echo our own unrecognized fears.

Would I ever be enthusiastic again?

My career as a psychotherapist covered nearly two decades. It took two degrees and tens of thousands of tuition dollars to place me in the therapist's chair. It wasn't quite burnout that motivated me to leave. However, I was feeling a little crisp around the edges. Managed care meant tons of unwelcome paperwork. My availability to clients lessened as I traveled to see grandchildren. Also a nagging sense kept surfacing that there was something else calling me. I took my own advice. It was time to risk. I began the transition from therapist to whatever would be next. On that day with Eileen I was still uncertain.

I was dangling.

Like a trapeze artist, I'd let go of one bar and was praying like hell there was another swinging toward me. Suspended. All I could see was an unknown future. That's how it feels when we move from the familiar to the unfamiliar. No matter the cause, cracking open brings us to a state of groundlessness. Trusting that we will eventually connect with *something* takes tremendous courage.

"This is my wife Nancy. She's *my* private psychotherapist." People would chuckle and Don would smile proudly at me. He liked being married to a therapist and enjoyed using his clever opening line. After I left my practice he asked, "How should I introduce you now?" Translation: "I knew what you used to be, but now what are you?" I felt sad, hearing the disappointment in his question. I said, "You can start by saying this is Nancy, my wife."

Pema Chodron, a Buddhist nun, has radical advice for us in her book, *When Things Fall Apart*. She says to remain there with as much curiosity and compassion as we can manage. "To stay with that shakiness—to stay with a broken heart, with a rumbling stomach, with feelings of revenge—that is the path of true awakening." I tried to keep this perspective. *It's a beginning. Most people don't have an opportunity to start anew.* But every fiber in my being wanted to disguise my discomfort and avoid uncertainty.

Is it valuable to crack open?

Partly, the timing of the inquiry will influence our answer. Asked in the midst of a life-splitting event, we may determine it's a worthless experience. Pain colors our response. With a longer perspective, we see value born out of suffering. Sometimes it takes someone from outside to identify what we're gaining. To the caterpillar, it looks like the end of the world. But as the chrysalis cracks we see it wasn't an ending—but the beginning of a butterfly. Friends or family may need to lend their perspective so that we see the boon in the transition. Otherwise, we're at risk of crying for our caterpillar self.

Einstein said that we have to answer one important question: *Do we live in a friendly or unfriendly universe?*

If we see the universe as a hospitable place, cracking open is part of our life cycle. It's similar to seeds that sprout only after their hull splits. We don't have a choice. Life opens us. Like Hemingway said: "The world breaks everyone and afterwards many are strong in the broken places." Our choice is how we respond to the experience. Will we let our pain count for something? This process may show us that we are not who we thought we were. It may also introduce us to dormant inner resources.

Our authenticity depends on how we meet these moments. We can deny what is happening and work at masking our broken-ness. In that view, breaking is shameful. It means we're flawed. But attempts to look good rarely work. Jung said that strangers see in a glance what takes us years to see about ourselves in therapy. We hide in glass closets. What we don't often appreciate is that brokenness can make us more human. Our weaknesses can draw others closer. Our drive for perfection often pushes them away. Look good or feel real?

That is the choice.

In *Eat, Pray, Love*, author Elizabeth Gilbert found words to describe the universal work of cracking open. With clarity and a wicked sense of humor she tells what happened when what she thought was true wasn't. Sobbing on her bathroom floor, she recognized the lie of her perfect life. "I was trying not to know this, but the truth kept insisting itself on me." We have all had or will have "bathroom floor moments." They can be as common as discovering we are not the wife, mother, or success we hoped to be, or as frightening as facing a serious illness or death. Or the end of a career path can break apart the life we thought we'd live forever.

Falling apart scares us to the bone. We also find it fascinating. It is a consistent storyline in most books and movies. Music, es-pecially country and western songs, would be lost without this theme. The blues just wouldn't exist without people being broken open and putting the pain to music. Magazines feature the celeb-rity of the month who is suffering from "exhaustion." Exhaustion has replaced the old code words "nervous breakdown" for a life in tatters. Marilyn Monroe had a nervous breakdown. Lindsay Lohan suffered from exhaustion. It became obvious that there was much more than tiredness plaguing her.

It's hard to imagine a life that doesn't unravel in some measure.

Yet we speak about these times as anomalies. As if they are avoidable. As if they are due to bad genes, bad luck, or bad karma. Surely, we think, alarming outcomes happen to the less deserving among us. The too wild, too rich, or too careless have lives that collapse. Not us.

When I look back over my own life, I see a series of events in which my life fell apart and came back together. Some big. Some small. Like my morning orange juice, I need a label that reads, "Reconstituted."

January in Tucson, Arizona is cold, especially at 6,875 feet. Kitt Peak National Observatory's buildings look like elongated igloos that poke up from the mountainsides. They house the largest collection of optical telescopes in the world. Each one reaches deep into the sky's secrets.

It's 5 a.m. My friend Donna and I spent a sleepless night stargazing. Jason, a young astronomer and our guide, deftly traced through the universe to show us stars, planets, and galaxies until dawn. "Donna, can you go to sleep now?" I ask, knowing I can't. We are both higher than the altitude. Mysterious visions dance in our heads. We saw places where stars die, stellar nurseries, swirling spirals of light, and the rings of Saturn. One cluster of stars, unromantically named M 14, looks like silvery diamonds sprinkled on a jeweler's cloth, the sky behind it a velvety indigo.

We are stardust. We are golden. We are two billion-year-old carbon... Joni Mitchell's words are both poetic and accurate. We *are* a collection of stardust. According to the European Space Agency, "Science is now confident that most of the atoms in our bodies and, indeed, in everything around us, were once in the hearts of stars."

Stars crack open and release carbon into the universe. Those atoms become us. One thing ends and something new begins.

For days after stargazing, each person I encounter appears as an intricate process. I can see them forming and falling apart in the dance of their lives. Not static beings. They are human happenings called Bob, Jeanie, or whatever. Light flickers, like stardust, in their eyes. It must be what Whitman felt when he wrote, "As to me I know of nothing else but miracles." I want to live in this awareness. But standing in line a few days later, I don't see developing humans, but people who are in my way. Rushing to God knows where, we have little patience for others and ourselves. Busyness blocks the truth.

As a therapist, I sat with clients while they sorted through their brokenness. It was often hard for them to imagine that they'd ever feel like their old selves. I knew they wouldn't. I also knew *that* was the good news. Their energy would return. They'd be engaged in their lives again, but something about them would be changed forever. If they stay vulnerable and touch the tender places, they'll discover more of their voice. Knowing this doesn't stop the ache, but it brings meaning to suffering.

Leading women's groups and teaching painting for self-expression gives me new ways to participate in the cracking open process. I know fear, pain, and confusion awaits us. But I also remember what the mystic Rumi said. *Don't turn away. Keep looking at the bandaged place. That's where the light enters you.* This is an invitation. If we look at the bandaged places our voice resonates from a deeper place—a truer place.

I now have a pair of earrings made of mermaid's tears. Once upon a time, the glass that forms them was part of a bottle. It sat on a drugstore shelf. Eventually it was trash. Tumbling and turning it ended up in the Pacific Ocean. A woman searching on Three Tree

Beach in Seattle finds the scattered pieces. She polishes them and then wraps them with wire. From fragments, she creates a thing of beauty.

This is life's pattern. Everything takes shape—cracks open—takes shape—cracks open.

Modern-day mystic and songwriter Leonard Cohen got it right when he sang, "That's how the light gets in."

Penguin

Holding On

*Embarking on the spiritual journey is like getting into a very small boat
and setting out on the ocean to search for unknown lands...*
Pema Chodron

I slipped a coin into my father's casket the day we buried him. A Spanish peseta imprinted with the head of King Juan Carlos on one side and a crown on the other. Soundlessly, it slid from my fingers and disappeared into a crevice of tufted satin. This token, made of copper and nickel, was a relic from my life-changing journey to Spain. I had carried it home like a beachcomber who brings a seashell back to a landlocked life in the hope it's charged with sea energy.

People have buried religious and utilitarian items with the deceased for centuries. It still happens. Even those I assume are above such superstitions can fall prey to this ancient practice. William F. Buckley's son sent the TV remote, a jar of peanut butter, and a rosary along with his famous dad in his casket. My own father was not what you would call a spiritual type. Sending any religious paraphernalia with him seemed insensitive. A Spanish coin was impractical. I was quite sure he wasn't headed to the Iberian Peninsula. Nor would he need pocket money.

Anyone who has lost a loved one knows of the temptation to retreat from this searing reality. Death pushes us into bouts of magical thinking as complex emotions overwhelm us. Bargains and fanciful side trips scatter grief's path. But sending this coin with my dad wasn't a death-denying deed. It was recognition of the hidden world my father entered. His soul, now released from his body, was traveling. I prayed that this coin, saturated with the energy of my homecoming, would help him find his way home. *Hold on to this,* I thought. *Wherever you go, hold on to this.*

Sometimes the best we can do is to hold on.

But what is it that we hold on to?

Author Anne Lamott held on to a blue shoe from a gumball machine during a particularly hard time in her life. "I couldn't put it down," she said. "Everywhere I went, I shoved it into my pocket; the friend I was staying with used to sort of laugh at me, but one day, something very sad happened in her life, and I left the blue shoe with a note for her by her coffee cup, that said I wished I could take the pain off her or carry it for her, but instead, I could just promise that I would walk through it by her side. She couldn't put it down."

It isn't the coin, blue shoe, or charm that gets us through. It's what it represents. Trinkets are stand-ins for the unseen things that comfort. These objects make the qualities of love, friendship, compassion, and solace visible. They provide something concrete to clutch when the floor has fallen out from under us. Charms and amulets might seem a strange topic in the pursuit of self-trust. But learning to trust ourselves often means letting go of how we've seen ourselves in the past. At the very least, this exploration shakes our sense of self. In the worst of times, it can feel like we are dying as we release a familiar self-image in order to discover more of who we are.

This letting go process leaves us searching for reassurance. The challenge when things fall apart is not to pull away from the situation, but to courageously ride through it. Sometimes it means finding a quality, a belief, or even a charm that can bring ease during a rough time. Talismans and trinkets are physical symbols that reassure and help us believe we can make it. And, in moments when we are lost, touching them reminds us of something that is bigger than our current circumstances.

It's an act of faith.

Theologian and author Mary Gordon says,

> *Without faith we would be paralyzed. We believe that all men are created equal. That our mothers, or at least our dogs, love us. That the number four bus will eventually come. All these represent a belief in the unseen. The question is not, then, are we people of faith, which we as a species seem to be. But rather, what then is the nature of that faith? And what actions does it lead to?*

It is odd that we rarely explore where we place our faith. If asked, "Do you believe in God?" we might answer quickly. But if we answer "yes" or "no," what does that response mean to us? Do we believe in one God or many? We avoid these questions. If pressed we might say, "I have my beliefs; just don't ask me to define them." But when our security is shaken we often reach out for something.

Rarely do we explore what it is that sustains us until we're faced with difficulties.

—⁓—

Confronting a crushing move from Indiana to Michigan in the middle of sixth grade, I looked for something to hold on to. God seemed so far away and I needed something immediate...something local.

For me it was a penguin....

Not a real one...

A brass penguin.

Guardian angels weren't part of our family's beliefs. But I certainly longed for their shelter. And in the absence of charmed cherubs, I discovered a small brass penguin. There he was, waiting for me on a knickknack shelf in our living room. He fit perfectly into my palm or slipped easily into a pocket. That enchanted penguin got me through the trauma of moving midyear. It was an all-around difficult time for me.

Most of my new classmates already had friendships developed over previous grades. My new teacher didn't like me or my Indiana twang. Mom was busy with a new baby. Changes in my body were perplexing. All that was familiar had vanished. Comfort of my childhood home, my perch in our peach tree, the shed that became a playhouse—all gone. Friendships that took years to build—all lost.

Holding that penguin let me believe I could make it through the ridicule of being the new kid and the disorientation distance created. His cool body resting in my pocket gave me tangible relief. In true magician style, when his mission was complete, he disappeared. Now like a forlorn lover, I occasionally think about him. Where is he? Is he tucked into the hand of some other little girl or sitting on a shelf with dusty bric-a-brac? I've searched for him in antique stores. I've perused eBay hoping I'll find him there.

In adulthood, our choices are often more sophisticated: A piece of art, music, a philosophy, or even a particular book can serve to reassure us. We may be unaware that it is comfort we seek when we reread an adored book. But books can console us. Oscar Wilde said, "If one cannot enjoy reading a book over and over again, there is no use in reading it at all." Familiar books bring solace to a disturbed life. They become amulet-like in their ability to reestablish a desired inner connection.

No matter how logical or scientifically trained we are, amulets can assist us in stressful situations. As astronaut Edward White II floated outside his Gemini 4 capsule, tethered by a 25-foot umbilical cord, he knew what was tucked in his pocket. Before he left Earth to become the first American spacewalker he'd slipped a St. Christopher's medal, a gold cross, and a Star of David into the right-hand pocket of his spacesuit.

Travel into space, over oceans, or even into unknown inner landscapes frequently produces anxiety. Early seafaring men feared encountering mermaids. Dread of these dangerous divas might sound foolish to us. But reported sightings and tales of ensnared sailors made this possibility believable. Maritime regulation took it seriously. As late as the 19th century, British law claimed that all mermaids found within their waters would be property of the Crown.

Sailors wore golden earrings as a safeguard. If captured, they'd use the jewelry as barter for their release. Only a foolhardy man went to sea without the price of liberty hanging from his earlobe. I can just imagine feeling that golden hoop hanging from an ear. It must have given them some relief. The perils of the sea were many. But they had protection from one of its dangers.

Outside my therapy office window was a huge blaze maple. Clients sat with their backs to it, facing me. Death of a loved one or divorce often brings people to therapy. They need something to hold on to. What's happening doesn't make sense. Realities they didn't want to consider do happen. Children die. Friends leave. Marriages end. It's easy to believe that we are safe from danger until loss bursts in like an unwanted visitor. Nothing makes sense.

Growth happens during disruptive times precisely because of our forced reexamination of what we believe. While listening to my clients and talking about what they faced, I often noticed the tree in the background. It was hard to miss. Outstretched branches filled my third floor window. The maple stood as silent witness to all that happened inside the room.

We formed a partnership, this trustworthy tree and I. I watched its rhythms and found its message reassuring—*everything changes— everything has a season*. Spring buds reminded me that warmer times were on the way. Summer breezes rippled through emerald waving hands, inviting play. Fiery fall colors dared me to look away. Branches full of blazing color gave way to grey simplicity. Leafless. Still. And when the inevitable snow gathered upon its pewter bones there was little evidence of life. But its energy continued to pulse through its core and reached deep into the earth.

Nature's patterns give us something to hold on to.

Bill Moyers asked author Margaret Atwood in an interview if she believed in the existence of the soul. She said, "Yes. It makes a better story." I love her reply. It's clear to me that the acknowledgment of soul changes the story of our lives. As a psychotherapist, I didn't talk about soul and spoke little about the spiritual life of clients. My training said it was out of bounds. Maybe this is why

I had to leave my practice, to find my *own* soul's voice. I needed settings where I could speak about other realities, to acknowledge unseen forces that give meaning to my life.

A changing sense of self is part of discovering our true voice. Panic often grabs us as our familiar self-image crumbles. In those panicky moments, we'll be left with important questions. What can I reach for when terror strikes? What's my connection to that invisible vital force that inhabits all living things? Is everything, others, nature and the cosmos, merely a backdrop for my life? What does it mean to have a soul? Psychiatrist Carl Jung said we only need to answer one key question:

"Am I related to something infinite or not?"

Well, are you?

Mountains

Living in Layers

What might my life be like were I to give in
to the rhythms of my own ragged dance?
Susan Hanson

*B*are feet thump on the yoga center's parquet floors. Kristi's drum vibrates with ancient beats. Women spin and spiral past me. They gaze inward—arms wide open in a welcoming gesture, palms turned up, as if to receive a blessing. We could be in a Turkish village, a Gypsy camp in Romania, or a mountain cave in southern Spain…it doesn't matter where. It doesn't matter who is watching. Job descriptions, family roles, and confining expectations fall from us like Salome's veils. We dance and greet aspects of ourselves rarely seen.

Arriving back home, I slip between the cool sheets and slide into the warm curve of Don's sleeping body. He whispers, *Hi, how was tonight?* Words can't explain it, I think. Silence. Then I begin to tremble. Shocked by my quivering body, I am speechless. Sobbing. Sobbing. Sobbing. *What brought this on?* he says rubbing my shoulder. He's perplexed. Nearly fifty years of bathing in my libidinal waters and my tears still puzzle him. Sometimes I am also uncertain about where they come from.

It is time to sleep but instead...

Tears flow down and soundless sighs come up from deep in my belly. I am five or fifteen or fifty. I am wise. I am innocent. I am mourning. Grief, cold and burning hot, grabs me. It lets me know just how long I've gone without letting the warmth of joy melt the icy grip numbing routine has on my heart.

Don is quiet.

Then I hear the reassuring pattern of his snoring.

I am silent, but restless—my first thought...

Escape to Colorado.

San Juan Mountains' strong arms will hold me. Cradled in their embrace, I am home. Mother Nature's mighty power is evident. Sitting on her rocks, climbing her cliffs, listening to her creeks, hearing her voice bubble with the thrill of living, I connect to my own untamed voice. There I feel what philosopher and Nobel prize-winner Rabindranath Tagore called "the life-throb of ages dancing in my blood."

But instead of escaping I fall asleep.

Usually when we think of slowing down it means becoming still. But there is another way. We can slow down by stepping out of habitual patterns. The desire to break free of deadening routines is what motivates thousands of comfy people to camp in less than comfortable conditions. Departure from the familiar brings new perspectives and a renewed appreciation of what we have or what we long for. While we women were spinning and spiraling at the yoga center our usual lives had stopped.

The next morning Don's question about where my tears came from is the focus of my writing. His inquiry and the dancing exposed a churning that had been with me for days—even decades.

Where did these tears come from?

Is last night the best place to look?

Or, do I go back to those early cutoff spots where I felt the excitement of summer at the edge of an Indiana creek? Maybe I weep for a Tom Sawyer girl who gleefully explores oozy mud that houses turtles and snakes while its waters slurp over rocks.

Why do I cry?

I cry because I want summer's joy to still fill me. Standing here at sixty-seven I wish to be the girl who knows life is just one long unfolding adventure. In girlhood moments of discovery we touch what saints and gurus teach—Life is one bite of baloney sandwich followed by a gulp of Cherry Kool-Aid.

Now as salty rivulets run down my cheeks I remember that looking back can be dangerous. Like Lot's wife, I could be on the road to somewhere and with a backward glance become as immobile as a pillar of salt.

But I want to look back—I want to remember.

I weep for the return of the untamed feminine. The goddess of the market, the beguiling mermaid of the ocean, the fairy in the garden, the muse in the kitchen, the wily witch stirring her fire, the temptress in the parlor and the sacred prostitute in her chamber, all have been banished to a distant land.

No longer welcome, they plead at our doors, "Admit me! Admit me! I am the one who holds the mysteries. I am the one who fills your breath with perfume. I'm the intoxication you wish to feel. Admit me! Admit me! I am the joy in your dancing and the grace of your steps. Admit me! Admit me!

I am the one who fills your heart with the beat of life.
Admit me!
Admit me!

The dancing broke open my awareness. I now look at the world in a whole new way. Feminine energy aches to dance free. It searches for potential passageways. Last night's dancing opened a portal.

In every decade of my adulthood I've worked to unleash this confined spirit. In the 1960s I thought sexual freedom would release her. In the 1970s it seemed to be political power and the passage of the Equal Rights Amendment. In the 1980s, I believed an advanced degree and a profession would liberate her. In the 1990s, I created programs supporting women to live their dreams. I believed this would encourage her spirit to dance free.

Celebrating the Maiden, Mother, and Crone as expressions of creativity's cycles led to retreats in the San Juan Mountains of Colorado. I formed groups to honor the wisdom of aging women. We sat in circles, telling our stories as rituals incubated in our collective womb of imagination. Now in the 2000s I facilitate ongoing women's circles to embody the feminine in our daily lives. Each of these is a response to a desire many women share with me.

We ache to come home to ourselves, blending the strength we gained with the softness that nurtures. Connecting heart and mind, we wish to create choices reflecting our deepest longing and best thinking. Vibrating with the timbre of our own powerful voices, we want our truth and wisdom to define our lives and contribute to our communities.

In the sixties I crossed a cultural divide. During my first years of marriage, women were primarily housewives. Über wives and career professionals began to replace the *just a housewife* role as we landed in the seventies. And while the promise was that we could be anything we wanted to be, some choices were not valued and were presented as less attractive. There is one undeniable fact: Sometimes we give up important aspects of ourselves in the name of growth. And at some point, we need to retrieve these aspects. As an adult I had to rediscover my childhood love of nature and my innate connection to wonder. As a *liberated* woman I need to reconnect with a deeper sense of the feminine.

Mothering our two young children in a tiny Cape Cod-style house, I was alone in a way I had never imagined. Saylor Street was lined with identical houses. Almost all of them contained a young family like ours. When mothers talked over the fence or a cup of coffee, we didn't talk about our feelings of isolation. We shared recipes and childcare woes. Our homes were just far enough apart to keep us from sensing one another's fears.

Betty Freidan said we had what is called "the problem without a name." When her words in *The Feminine Mystique* reached my eyes I was thrilled.

I was found.

I couldn't wait to tell Don about my discovery.

Shaving his boyish face, Don completed the daily ritual of preparing to enter the world of men and metal. I squeezed into the tiny bathroom unable to wait another minute to begin reading to him. Precariously perched on the edge of the bathtub, I shared excerpts from Freidan's book. I was the image of two colliding worlds. One world was represented by the tightly held book. My outfit was a symbol of the other. Purple polyester with paisley print formed a dress that scarcely covered my tush. White glossy patent leather boots hugged my feet before crawling over my calves to end at my kneecaps. What a picture I must have been as I read these words...

The problem lay buried, unspoken… Each suburban wife struggled with it alone. As she made the beds, shopped for groceries, matched slipcover material, ate peanut butter sandwiches with her children, chauffeured Cub Scouts and Brownies, lay beside her husband at night—she was afraid to ask even of herself the silent question—"Is this all?"

I looked up from the page in horror at the life I had been living. I am a cupcake in lilac and white, who sees a chance at new life. "I can't go on living like this," I proclaim to the back of Don's head and his frothy reflection. His razor glides in measured strokes as he squeezes out his reply from an oddly shaped mouth, "Why Not?"

"Well for one thing, what would it be like if I dressed this way at fifty?" I replied, struggling to impress him with my need to change. "What would be wrong with that?" He said, rinsing foam from his Gillette and cleanly shaven face. "I'd be a woman in girl's clothing," I said, realizing that this sounded like more of a problem for me than for him.

Change was happening.

I felt it.

I didn't have words for it.

But it was on its way.

I began, almost from that bathroom moment, to reshape my life. I was drunk with the power of new choices. I began to smoke small cigars, attended formal events in trousers, carried a briefcase, and passed out business cards. All of this, to prove I was somebody. I ignored the warning that anthropologist Ashley Montagu gave to burgeoning feminists. He said, "If you are in a war, you don't take on the weaknesses of your opponent." His message was to honor the strengths women have. Although it made sense, I still believed that if I did what men did I'd be valued.

Friedan's inquiry had exposed one problem: *Is that all there is?* That question got women thinking. We looked out of our spotless windows and saw possibilities: education, new careers, and a chance to have it all. College was not an option I had previously considered. But in 1970 I enrolled in a community college, along with tens of thousands of other women across America.

There was a deeper, less evident question that wasn't answered back then. It didn't appear for decades. *How do we honor and embrace feminine energy in all of its forms?* That is the challenge we face now. Its resolution has far-reaching implications for both men and women.

⁕

Decades later, this time in an elegant hotel restroom, I stand chatting with two women. We're on break from a networking event. Professional personas begin dropping faster than rose petals in September. Barb, a CPA, Carol, an attorney for a multinational law firm, and me, a psychotherapist, talk about sewing...of all things. Barb says, "I love to sew but I just don't have time. I feel strange even talking about it, like it's old-fashioned and depicts me as somehow less powerful. So I never mention it at the office. But I do miss it." Carol and I nod in recognition. Why is it embarrassing? What is wrong with sewing as a hobby? Martha Stewart can talk about sewing all she wants. She turned feminine crafts into a million dollar empire and that legitimized it... at least for her.

It is okay to talk about sewing for profit— just not for pleasure.

As Barbara Kingsolver pointed out in *Animal, Vegetable, Mineral,* somewhere along the way we swapped something precious for things of lesser value.

When we traded homemaking for careers, we were implicitly promised economic independence and worldly influence. But a devil of a bargain it has turned out to be in terms of daily life. We gave up the aroma of warm bread rising, the measured pace of nurturing routines, the creative task of molding our families' tastes and zest for life; we received in exchange the minivan and the Lunchable.

In that trade we learned the language of business and sometimes struggled with the overt use of our power. We uncovered limits that are both internal and cultural. Making ourselves heard did happen in boardrooms, offices, and shops. Yet, even as we made progress, intuitively we felt something cherished was being lost. Maybe this had to happen. Abundant lives now allow us to listen for the call of a deeper, richer voice.

We are daughters rummaging through our mother's lives looking for clues. What are the lessons and warnings their stories possess? Women tell me they want work that uses all their talents and relationships that reveal the passion they yearn to express. They are looking for what was left back there, before the appearance of Lunchables and the minivans.

They search for something that has not yet been fully revealed. Artist Georgia O'Keeffe must have sensed this also when she said, "I feel there is something unexplored about women that only a woman can explore." In that exploration, I believe we'll discover that what we once thought was unimportant has great value.

Naomi Wolf, a self-proclaimed feminist, political consultant, and author of multiple books, said on a recent book tour that planting a basil garden left her feeling anxious. "Shouldn't I be doing something more useful?" She'd honed her analytical abilities for years and in the process something important had died. This is how she saw it. "I started my life as a poet, but along the way I'd lost my connection to my imagination."

As bare feet slid across the wooden floors at the yoga center I rediscovered something of what I lost—a connection to my own imagination. Our dancing is what economist, author, and political advisor Jeremy Rifkin calls "deep play." It can take many forms; planting a basil garden, painting, sewing, writing poetry, photography, cooking, or any other activity that results in joy. It is made up of pursuits that bring pleasure without the burden of making a profit. For most women I know, endeavors for the sake of joy alone are rare.

Deep play reconnects us to our souls.

When bestselling author Oriah Mountain Dreamer attended a church service, she was surprised by her reaction to an arrangement of the 23rd Psalm by singer and songwriter Bobby McFerrin. His version, dedicated to his mother, ends by replacing Father, Son, and Holy Ghost with Mother, Daughter, and Holy of Holies. Oriah says in a recent blog post, "I was stunned to find my eyes filling with tears...There is a great loss if our circle of caring for the world does not encompass all aspects of ourselves, including our gender, the particular form the Mystery takes for a short while..."

Oriah's words are with me as I step into my garden. A lemon-yellow butterfly, with delicate veins of ebony outlining its wings, lands on a bright pink coneflower. The contrast makes me catch my breath. Motionless. I hardly breathe as I try to take in this astonishing beauty. I am filled with questions. *What creates things of this splendor? What energy is loose in the world, taking so many forms in so many hues and patterns?* Butterflies and mountains are outward and visible reminders of the creative spirit that runs through all of life. Surely there must be a place for the touch of a feminine hand in all of this.

Our son Doug was in the Air Force during Desert Shield. He was stationed in Saudi Arabia. I met him at the kitchen door the day he returned. I cried soulful tears not unlike my tears on that night of dancing. They flowed from me as my fears for his safety could finally be released. I also cried from the joy of seeing him again. I let him go only because others were waiting to greet him. He was then reunited with his father, sister, aunt, and uncle. All stood nearby ready to give him a heartwarming bear hug. Then it was time to celebrate. The food came out, the feasting began, laughter returned, and we regaled each other with stories.

Like absent loved ones, forgotten feminine aspects have to be recollected. They need to be gathered up and brought back home to our daily lives. This process will involve tears. And after the tears, it will be time to embrace and celebrate the feminine as we connect with her strength, tenderness, and beauty. In those moments bliss will spread through our bodies like warm sunshine.

⸱⸱⸱

Reclining goddesses are easy to imagine in the curves and valleys of the San Juan Mountains. The earth rounds and slopes like bellies and breasts. Gigantic female bodies stretch out in all directions. Quaking and shaking brought these mountains into being. They were rumbaed into place by a fiery dance. Cracks and breaks remind us where that movement occurred. Fleshy mountainsides of red rock have stripes of white and green, along with shades of pink and orange. Each color marks a different event in their lives.

Mountains form in layers.

Mountains with their distinctive younger sections stacked above the basement rock remind me of my own layered life. We each have transitions that leave their marks. Looking back we can see distinct *geological shifts* and the traces they leave.

The tomboy me loved nature and found living in the moment easy. The young mother in purple and white awoke to her own power and talents. The professional psychotherapist reached out to others while moving away from things like sewing that seemed unacceptable. The dancing me is the searcher who longs for a more encompassing feminine model to inhabit. These are the stages of one woman's life.

Our lives, like the lives of mountains, have layers.

This same sense must have been what seventy-year-old poet laureate Stanley Kunitz felt when he wrote his poem entitled "The Layers."

I have walked through many lives
some of them my own
and I am not who I was
though some principle of being abides
from which I struggle not to stray.

He reminds us that while many changes and shifts take place in a lifetime we need to stay in touch with the unfolding mystery at the heart of life.

This time I've returned to the San Juan Mountains with four granddaughters in tow. Sprinkled in ages from eight to almost sixteen, someday they will look back upon their own lives of layered womanhood. As their grandmother, my wish for them is what I hope for all of us: May we honor and embrace feminine energy and recognize it as one form the Great Mystery takes in the dance of life. And may we all have the courage to give in to the rhythms of our own ragged dance.

Dish Soap

Tumbling Awake

I love myself when I am laughing. And then again
when I am looking mean and impressive.
Zora Neale Hurston

*M*arch morning. Birds beckon. Sun barely up. My schedule is as clear as Martha Stewart's windows. I turn off the phone. Grab my coffee, journal, and pen. I settle into my chair. My ideas are popping. Writing will fill every delicious moment of my day.

Don is leaving for the office and a business dinner afterwards. His plans ensure that it will be easy to follow my own rhythm. His goodbye includes a request. "Honey, will you copy these papers and drop them off at the tax guy's office today?" Two folders each about an inch thick are pregnant with papers. He lays them on the desk next to my journal and pen. I'm in shock. I rustle through the stacks in horror. Many of these sheets are printed on both sides. This stack is actually even bigger than it appears.

I panic.

When I have my day planned it's hard for me to make last minute changes. Even little ones seem intrusive. This change is a two to three hour interruption that includes tedious copying and a disruptive drive to the accountant's office. Which means getting out of my PJs and putting on makeup or at the very least washing my face.

His request is fair.

Unfortunately, the reasonable part of me was unavailable for comment.

I respond with the ferociousness of a mother bear protecting a cub, or in this case her precious writing time.

"I CAN'T! I HAVE MY WHOLE DAY PLANNED! THIS WILL TAKE HOURS! I HATE LAST MINUTE CHANGES!"

He looks stunned.

After I calm down we begin to work out a compromise. It turns out that the next day is just as good. "I'll do it tomorrow," I tell Don. He leaves apparently satisfied. Reverberations from my first response are undoubtedly still ringing in his ears.

Now back to writing… well… well…

…my momentum is gone.

I've lost the beat.

Our resolution hasn't freed me.

My attention is still stuck to his request like a fly on flypaper.

Somebody told me that obstacles could be gifts. Difficulties slow us down. They make us look at things in a new way. This purveyor of wisdom forgot to add that it's hard to appreciate this while you're tumbling through the air. The value of an obstacle is seen best from a distance...a long distance.

Now I'm tumbling—not writing.

What's the problem, I wonder. *I have the house to myself, nowhere to go, and nothing to do but write. Maybe eating a snack will help settle me. Or a few minutes of the news would be good about now?* Apparently the conflict is no longer between Don and me. It has taken up residence in my head. It's now between me and me. I should have taken care of Don's request. *Shouldn't I have?* Here is the ugly truth: I had an expectation... I wanted *him* to know how important this day was for me. Couldn't he just see how engaged I was in writing and not ask me to run this errand? And as author Anne Lamott points out, "expectations are resentments under construction."

Now rather than writing, I'm doing mini-psychotherapy and consciousness-raising on myself. *It's all right to blow it once in a while! Nobody's perfect. Women need to speak up for what they want and need. You can't expect him to read your mind.*

None of this helps.

Losing my focus disappoints me. I'm ashamed of my graceless response. I'm sitting here with a lapful of guilt. *You teach "I" statements,* my inner critic says, drumming her fingers on the desk. *For God's sake, you communicate for a living!* Remember how to do it? *I feel frustrated when you make last minute requests without considering my schedule.* Well, something like that might have worked.

Then it dawns on me—this is a dilemma for many women. We think the real measure of who we are is the state of our relationships. If things are going well with family, friends, or colleagues that means we're okay. If not—Angst... Turmoil... Uneasiness. *I'd rather have a harmonious relationship than stir things up by asking for what I want,* is what some women tell me. They stifle their voice because of the hassle. To say *I am here and this is what I need* isn't easy.

Stating our needs doesn't ensure that we'll feel better imme-diately. It isn't a cure for anxiety. In fact, often it can make us feel more anxious. Because humans are tension-avoiding animals, we look for expedient resolutions to move out of distress as quickly as possible. This is understandable. However, it can mean giving up on us. If, rather than doing what we planned, we fill their requests to run the errand, clean up after them, or compile their report, the tension will subside. The unpleasant conflict fades. But it is a temporary resolution. We have sidestepped the situation, not solved it. Worse yet, we send a message to others and ourselves that what we need isn't important.

When I read the following quote by David Richo in his book *Shadow Dance*, I understood why we have such a hard time figur-ing out what it is that we want. "Not to know what I want is a sign that I am not living in my true self more than half the time." Repeatedly acting without considering our own longings discon-nects us from our authentic selves. Eventually, what we do stops reflecting who we are. When someone does ask us what we want, our eyes meet theirs with a blank stare. We really no longer know. Our enthusiasm leaves. Our body feels heavy. It takes all our energy to drag ourselves from place to place.

Over the last two decades, I've worked with women to clarify their dreams and goals. Many women tell me, "I don't know if I have a dream. I have no clue what I want." When we repeatedly defer to the needs of another, we lose the trail that leads to our own desires. I'm afraid that our unwillingness to stay present to conflicts is why so many of us say we don't know what we want. If we let ourselves know, we increase the potential for discomfort. Navigating our needs within relationships is a kind of tug-of-war. Too frequently, we let go of our end of the rope. By dropping it, we avoid feeling the tension created by pulling back.

There are still prohibitions against women speaking up. We have to find the ones we harbor and see how they chip away at our confidence. Here are some of the typical things that hide in our description of what it means to be a good woman: "Asking for what you want is self-centered." "Good women put others first." "You can't be nurturing and assertive." We need to remember that suppression is often an inside job. It's risky to step out not knowing where our foot will land. It might land in our mouth. But what if it does?

It won't be fatal.

If we stay with this inquiry, we can learn a great deal about ourselves. The hardest part is staying with the inner turmoil. We don't like what it stirs up. Doubt… Unworthiness… Unfamiliarity. This desire for peace pushes us to settle without exploring what is possible. Speaking up is what strengthens our voice and our relationships. It makes perfect sense. To know ourselves, to connect with others—we communicate. But that means periods of upheaval.

When we do speak up, we discover the value of tumbling.

———

A woman comes home from work and finds a pithy note on the kitchen counter. It's in her husband's handwriting. It says, "There is no Joy." She's shocked and consumed with worry. She knows their busy schedules have meant less time together. Had he seemed distant lately? He was working more hours. She has a demanding new job. What's troubling him? *I haven't been paying much attention to what he needs*, she thought.

She begins making his favorite meal while waiting for him to come home. When he returns, her enthusiastic welcome seems to puzzle him. After they sit down at the table she looks into his eyes and says in a quiet voice, "I got your note."

He says, "Oh, you did? I just wanted to remind one of us to pick up dish soap. I used what was left last night."

There is no Joy.

This is a funny story. I don't even know if it is true. If so, it's a great opening for them to laugh about the misinterpretation and talk about how they are doing with each other. But what I love about this anecdote is how it demonstrates the default position of many women's minds. There must be something wrong with the relationship. What can I do to understand it, clarify it, make it better… Also, her response to the note implies she is thinking, *I did something wrong, I have a problem, it must be my fault.*

What had she planned to do that evening before she found the note? We don't know. But women allow the needs of others to trump their own needs—repeatedly. No matter how practiced we are at self-assertion, the impulse to care for others is never far away. Maybe she had planned a soothing bath, a night of nurturing herself after the demands of her new job. Baths for many women are a place where they find tranquility. It's where they can be themselves and let the needs of others fade.

And bathing reminds me of one of my favorite mermaid myths from the 13th century:

Once upon a time and long ago there was a woman who, through no fault of her own, lived under a spell. Every Saturday night she turned into a mermaid. She knew this would be a problem once she married. But when her dream-man appeared, she convinced herself it could work. "I must bathe once a week in seclusion," she said, accepting his proposal. He thought, "This is a small request." It was true that she had recently helped him out of a life-threatening situation. This was the least he could do for her.

And so they married.

Every Saturday she sequestered herself. Her splendid mermaid tail unfurled and flopped over the tub and onto the floor. In time, he became curious. His friends questioned her behavior. What was she doing? Why couldn't he be present? What was she hiding? Was she really in there alone?

At last, it was too much for the guy. He had to know. Just a glimpse through the keyhole would answer his nagging fears. But she was an enchanted woman, and the instant his glance fell upon her scaly skin—she felt it.

Outraged, she shrieked, "Can't I ever have a minute to myself?"

I changed the ending. In the original myth she also has wings and flies out the window, abandoning him and their children. I like my closing. It reminds me that we often have to ask more than once. Clearly stating what we want doesn't mean it will always be remembered. Ask and then ask again. It takes courage and persistence to take ourselves seriously.

Fluffy-headed peonies that in May were a progression of crimson and pink are long gone. Coneflower's fuchsia petals of July have given way to dusty tones in August. Floribunda rosebushes continue to push blossoms of cream, pink, and scarlet onto thorny branches. Their ruffles of color are a special delight as other plants fade in late summer.

From my perch on the porch I watch the cycles of the seasons. I listen. I write. Paying attention is how my mornings begin now. I hear life around me and in me. Writing is now my practice of awareness. It helps me connect to the world and myself. The value of it is evident to me. My writing time is also evident to Don. I have made it clear over and over again by requesting that he respect it.

It's been years since my tumbling March morning. Now, looking back, I understand the lesson. My reaction to Don's proposed errand reflected my own uncertainty about my right to write. I was not convinced that taking this time for myself was legitimate. That is why the conflict found such a welcoming place inside of me.

Spending time doing what we desire builds a nest in our true selves. It lets us remember where we do belong. As David Richo indicates, to know who we are and what we want, fifty percent of the time we need to be living in our true selves. That means following the heart's tug even when someone else is pulling us in another direction.

Sometimes what our soul needs is in direct opposition to what others need. How do we stay true and honor our relationship to others? We stand in our own flipflops and ask, *How is this for me? Can I do this in a way that honors both of us?* True selves long for expression. This yearning lives in both men and women. It is bound to give rise to conflicts. Learning to speak with authenticity is often messy, awkward, and requires repeated attempts.

But it is worth it—

So worth it.

Hot Coffee

Ignoring the Muse

Now I understand that there is more to fear by ignoring this muse creature.
It's akin to ignoring who you really are.
Sunni Brown

*S*aturday morning. Journal and pen lie on the floor next to my bed. A line of poetry flirts with me. It begs me to write it down. *But first I must create a nest,* I think, jumping out of bed and heading downstairs to the kitchen. I load a tray with more pens, books, a mug and carafe of coffee, then make my way back to the waiting bed.

I then arrange everything on the bed and settle down in the center. There are plenty of pillows to prop me up in just the right position. *One more thing,* I think; *the phone, it needs to be handy.* I lean over to the nightstand and grab it—in case someone calls. This tips over the carafe.

Puddles of coffee soak the sheets. OH, #★#@★&, escapes from my mouth as I jump out of bed. Pens, books, mug, and pillows fly through the air. I feel like a crazed juggler.

Another chain of words escape from my mouth that I wouldn't want my granddaughters to say or hear. I grab the sheets and mattress cover. They are drenched. I race to the bathroom to throw them into the tub. Cold water soaked washcloth in hand, I return hoping to salvage the mattress…too late. Stubborn stains defy my efforts.

Off to the laundry room to wash the sheets, blankets, and mattress cover. With everything in the washer I return to the kitchen and make another pot of coffee. My daughter calls and we catch up on family news.

I unload and load the dishwasher.

I sit down at the computer in the family room. My bed is no longer an option, since it is unmade and wet from the coffee calamity. I have no idea what I was excited to write two hours ago. I might as well check email and pay bills.

Where did my muse go? Was she bored by my dawdling ways? Or did my muse leave when I showed no reverence for the words she hung before me like tiny prayer flags?

Contrast my response to American poet Ruth Stone's reaction to inspiration. She told Elizabeth Gilbert, author of *Eat, Pray, Love*, that as a child working in the fields of her family home in Virginia she remembers feeling the approach of a poem. "I can hear it thundering toward me from across the landscape, and all I can do is run like hell to get a pencil to capture it before it barrels on past and finds another poet." She knew, even at a young age, that inspiration is fleeting.

We have a choice when the muse appears. We can follow or ignore her. And there are many ways to ignore the muse. *First I must make a studio or a place to create before I can begin. I'll jot down my ideas after I do the dishes, clean the bathtub, and run to the store. Or I must make sure everyone else is taken care of before I paint.* But the Muse is fickle. She does not wait around for us to be ready. If we are blessed with a visitation from the muse we'd best be grateful and act accordingly.

Poet Stanley Kunitz said inspiration comes from what he called *wilderness.* It is that untamed part of us that births new creations. Decades of work led him to say, "The more you believe in its existence and know it walks with you, the more available it becomes and the doors open faster and longer. It learns you are a friendly host." Looking at my reaction to the muse that morning, it's clear that I was an ambivalent hostess. Both Stone and Kunitz tell us to treat the muse with reverence and respect. We need to prove by our actions that we are interested in what that whispered voice has to say.

When the muse is nearby we often tremble. That is because she calls us into the wilderness. Moving into the unknown excites and scares us. Who knows what we might discover there? Unpredictability is a basic ingredient of creativity.

If we make the creative process a part of our lives, we give up having the answers and begin to embrace curiosity. Sometimes I wonder, "How might my life change if I really trusted this place?" And that uncertainty is why my prayer to live more creatively sounds something like this… *Lord let me be more spontaneous—just don't let me mess up my comfortable life in the process.*

Werner Herzog, film director and producer, offers a glimpse of the earliest known cave paintings in his film, *Cave of Forgotten Dreams.* The caves, located about four hundred miles outside Paris, house artwork that is nearly thirty thousand years old. In flickering torchlight the camera reveals something that is distant yet familiar.

Mixed in with a menagerie of animal images are multiple red handprints.

I imagine a woman with red pigment on her hand as she places it on those cold limestone walls. Her breath quickens as she lifts it to see the shape that appears. Her eyes are full of wonder as she views her creation. Ancient crimson handprints express the same primal desire that lives in each of us—the ache to express who we are.

Longing like hers is part of the human experience in all cultures and throughout recorded history. The desire to make something, to leave our mark, plays an important part in helping us understand ourselves. Self-discovery is often enhanced by creative acts. The question then is: Why do we so often avoid it? We ignore creativity's tug for just that reason…it asks us to move into an unfamiliar sense of who we are.

When I asked a woman I know why she wasn't painting, even though she talks often about how much she longs to paint, she replied, "Honestly, it's not how I measure what's important. Completing my 'to do' list is what counts." She wasn't happy when she realized this. And if we are candid with ourselves we might also be shocked by what we use to measure our worth. Often creative endeavors are seen as fluff between the important things we do. Yet, creativity sustains us. It lets our souls breathe.

Do we really want our lives measured by completed errands on a list? On a daily basis it may appear that it is better to do the dishes, return calls, or pick up the dry cleaning. But over the course of a life, writing a poem is important also. We don't need to design an elaborate place to capture these whispers. The trick is staying out of the way and recognizing the truth of these moments. This is a lesson that I learn and relearn.

What might I have written that morning? I will never know. Why didn't I just reach for my journal and pen? Some of the time we fear being swept away in inspiration's capricious energies. When the muse has her way with me I have stopped caring about piles of unopened mail on the desk, stacks of dishes in the sink, or whether I wash my face and brush my hair.

Following inspiration's call changes lives. Maybe you long to open a boutique, create a program for pregnant teens, or take a painting class. Each of these longings will require you to grow in a unique way. It isn't just that a new business or lifestyle shifts our perspective. It can. But it's more than that. Taking action, especially actions with an uncertain outcome, demonstrates that we believe in ourselves. It affirms that our voice, gifts, and talents are worth expressing.

Honoring inspiration's call *is* transformative.

The "I'll do it later" response is a proven way to lose momentum. And the things we will get back to later, but never do, steal our enthusiasm. They rob us of motivation and the pleasure of accomplishment. As author and creativity researcher Rollo May said, "If you do not express your own original ideas, if you do not listen to your own being, you will have betrayed yourself. Also, you will have betrayed your community in failing to make your contribution." That is hard to hear. Most of us are so busy doing the things that are required to keep a family and career going that this can sound like an added burden. But it is a truth that we all must confront.

It is spring and my garden is waking up. Everything is stirring. Something begins to stir inside of me also. Flirtatious violets and exuberant daisies call out to be adored. Even the pebbles that surround the pond speak to me as they crackle under my feet. Each tiny stone reminds me that a garden is a holy place. Spring's message is clear as I stand here: "Open to the beauty that is around you and within you."

Rose canes stretched over the front door are coming to life. Leafy branches that cradle rosebuds have begun to emerge. One by one the flower's scarlet petals will unfold. The sun will nudge each rose until it is awake. In mid-June they will twirl open and be breathtaking against the white doorframe.

We are born into the same world as these roses. And like them we are in a process of unfolding—one petal at a time.

The morning of my coffee calamity, I *felt* a line of poetry nearby. It was different from having an idea for a poem. What makes inspiration unlike a good idea is that inspiration comes through us. We receive it. It is visceral. That is why trusting the process is important. Often our thinking self has to move over while we dive in. This willingness to plunge into the depths of the unknown led Bohemian diarist Anais Nin to say, "I must be a mermaid.... I have no fear of depths and a great fear of shallow living."

Creating a nest moved me away from the spark of inspiration into a strategy. These actions shut off my receptivity. My inner file clerk, she who likes to organize things and fears uncertainty, grabbed control. The next thing I knew it was two hours later. What did I have to show for my morning?

Coffee stains.

Frustration.

We know the ache to press our hand against the walls of our own caves. We long to see the mark we'd leave. When we dare, we awaken to our fullness. Inspiration's spark is in all of us. It is there for a reason. It's an invitation to co-operate in our own unfolding process. That is *why* it lives in each of us. We can participate in our own unfolding by listening and respecting that urge.

The twelfth-century Persian poet Hafiz described this awakening in his poem, "It Felt Love": "How did the rose ever open its heart and give to this world all its beauty? It felt the encouragement of light against its being. Otherwise, we all remain too frightened." He captured both the desire and the need for warmth as we open. And he acknowledged that without tenderness we would be too afraid to bloom.

Inspiration calls with a thought, an insight, a dream, or even a line of poetry. If we follow it, something new comes alive and our potential is revealed. We can feel both fear and excitement in these moments. Each time the same choice is there—do we open or pull away? To say "yes" to the muse takes courage because we don't know what that "yes" will reveal. We *can* be sure that to pay attention to her is a way of honoring who we truly are.

It is risky.

Can you feel a stirring to explore your inner wilderness?

Will you?

Do you dare?

Gypsy

Daring the Edge

The authentic self is the soul made visible.
Sarah Ban Breathnach

*L*iquid sapphire waters of the Atlantic Ocean surround me. Like a mermaid, I sit perched on huge grey boulders that are scattered along the coast of Finisterra, Spain. This tiny fishing village's name translates to "end of the earth." Once this rocky border was where the world stopped. It takes courage and the belief in a new possibility to sail into an abyss fully aware you might drop off the edge. Traveling into the unknown is the voyage I took.

I dared the edge.

The moon is faintly visible. In eight hours my family will see it. Back home, thousands of miles from here, they are in the middle of their day. Don, my husband, is at work. Our children, Doug, who's fourteen, and Debbie, twelve, are in school. They are going about their everyday lives. I wonder what they are doing this very moment.

Soon they will be in Spain with me. But for now I am here alone finishing my bachelor's degree; a researcher studying women's roles; a gypsy wandering through Spain; a woman looking for her voice. I am the reverse of the fabled *Little Mermaid*. She gave up her voice to have a different life. I temporarily gave up my life to find my voice.

Sometimes life grabs us. Before we realize it we are talking about taking outrageous steps. Yet this didn't happen quickly. After a year of negotiating and compromising, I left with one suitcase, a backpack, and my journal. If a young mother ever wants to amaze herself with all she does, she should write her job description. She'd be shocked by what it would take for someone to fill her shoes. I was. My list was impressive. And it didn't even cover everything I did on any given day.

Here's what I wrote: *shop for and prepare meals, wash dishes and clothes, run errands, nurse sick children, listen to hurt feelings, supervise homework, and my least favorite role—be on call as head referee.* Don's work of sixty-plus hours a week and the occasional business trip mean he'll need lots of help if I am not there.

Most of my college peers are at least ten years younger than me and are unmarried. They are perfectly suitable fulltime nannies for our children. But as I tell them what's expected, the job sounds overwhelming. One by one, they roll their eyes as if to say, "You must be kidding." Yet, I do all of it while attending college classes and having a part-time job.

Karen is perfect. She's a strident feminist. And as a supporter of women's rights, she thinks I am making a statement by going to Spain for three months on my own. We've shared a few classes over the last year or so. She always signs her notes to me, *Yours in the Struggle.* She's twenty, single, and I trust her. In class she demonstrates that she's responsible, likeable, and smart.

When she says "yes," I am relieved.

But a couple of months before my departure to Spain, Karen calls. "I can't stay with your kids. There is no way to do what you do and have a life," she says apologetically. I respond with a half-hearted, "That's okay." But it isn't okay. I close the bedroom door and lie across the bed crying. *I spent nearly a year, endlessly talking with Don, considering what it would cost financially and emotionally for our family—with one phone call it all falls apart.*

The idea of a semester abroad came out of the ether. One day I stopped to read a bulletin board on the way to a sociology class. I'd passed this sign many times. But this time I looked at the pictures of the students' faces and read the poster's bold print. It said, "STUDY ABROAD." *Ya, sure,* I thought. *I'm a 34-year-old undergraduate, a wife, and mother of two children. Not exactly the profile of an exchange student. This program is for young, single people…not me. I wish I could but I can't.*

Then a voice inside of me whispers, *Why not?*

That whispered "why not" reignites my love of anthropology and fantasy of being Margaret Mead. It affects me so profoundly that I mention it to Don that very night after dinner. "It could work," I tell him. "I'll spend three months in a remote village and study Mayan culture while improving my Spanish." I imagine writing pithy notes about women's roles in an isolated area of the Yucatan. He imagines me with dysentery, no health care, and unable to call home. "No," he says "I can't stand the thought of it."

"How about Spain?" I offer days later. My project will shift to women's changing roles in post-Franco Spain. It's still my area of study and I will improve my Spanish.

⸻

Snow stands in six-foot piles on either side of our front door. January's blizzard left twenty inches of the fluffy white stuff—more followed. It wasn't just precipitation that set records in 1979. Chicago also broke the record for below-zero days. On February 10th of that frosty year we pile into Don's car and head for O'Hare Airport. Don, Doug, and Deb will return to this igloo of a house…without me.

I want to be as frozen as the heaps of snow that cover the streets. I don't want to experience how painful this is for the three of them. But I do feel. Saying goodbye at the boarding gate is worse than I imagined. Feeling pulled in two different directions is familiar to most mothers. But never was my inner conflict as acute as it is now looking into my children's eyes Unmistakably, I am choosing what I want even though I know they want me to stay. I am the cause of the pain I see as tears run down Debbie's cheeks.

For nearly four months I would not tuck them under warm blankets on snowy nights. I wouldn't be there in the morning to kiss them in the moments of early morning tenderness. I wouldn't be there for quiet talks with Deb or to laugh as Doug demonstrates his gift of droll humor. I know that I am not supposed to leave my children. They should leave me on some far-off day when they are old enough to care for themselves. But leave I did.

I am a mother who went AWOL.

As Danish philosopher Kierkegaard said, "Life can only be understood backwards; but it must be lived forward." In choosing to leave I faced the dilemma so many of us do. How do we stay true to ourselves and faithful to those we love? It takes work… It takes perseverance and lots of honest talking. In this instance, we also had a little divine intervention. Just after Karen called and the trip fell apart, Marie appeared. Our minister's mother-in-law, she's a woman our family knows well. At 67, a retired English teacher of children the ages of Doug and Debbie, she's looking for a place to stay while her senior housing is completed.

The dates that she requires line up perfectly with my absence. We can help her as she helps us. We offer a place to stay and a small stipend. She accepts. Her maturity and teaching skills make her a much better choice than a twenty-year-old college student. She is such an accomplished teacher that Debbie and Doug's grades actually improve while I am in Spain.

In Spain, as I interviewed women about the pressures of their cultural expectations, my own life came into focus. I'd followed cultural cues as I graduated from high school, became a hairdresser, married, and at twenty-one became a mother. Yes, these choices were happy ones. But when the pressure from a culture is dictating a single outcome, the idea that we are the chooser is lost. Going to college was helping me look at options I'd never considered. Studying in Spain meant challenging the edge of what was acceptable for a wife and mother. Some would still say that I'd gone over the edge.

Even though it was something that Don and I worked out, many others had great difficulty with it, including our families. My father said I should be taken out behind the barn and spanked. A colleague of Don's actually told him to keep me away from his wife. I guess he was afraid that spirited ideas are contagious. Leaving was a challenge on many levels. I'd only been out of the country two times. Once with my parents to see Niagara Falls from the Canadian side. And once, Don and I vacationed in the Bahamas. Leaving for Spain was dramatic.

My determination to be authentic was greater than even I recognized. Being away I had no one to blame if things didn't go well. No one to get in the way of what I said I wanted to do. I was with myself in a way that I had never been. In the middle of my stay, swept up in Spain's Easter Pageantry, I thought, *It's improbable that I am up all night, drunk on ceremonies, chocolate, and churro. But here I am. I've crossed over some line I never thought I'd cross. I let my dream become my direction.* I did not come to Spain to improve my Spanish. I came to find my voice and save my soul.

I needed to return to a place in me that I forgot was there. That can mean, as actress Annette Bening says, "fumbling around and trying to say... Is this my voice? Is this who I am?" We all need to return to our soul's home from time to time. Because separation from our essence takes its toll on us—that's the overarching message. Regardless of how bright, cheery, and comfortable we have it. Regardless of the love, appreciation, or admiration we receive from others. Despite our accomplishments or competencies, disruption from what sustains withers the soul. A juicy life requires we connect with the deepest places at our core and attend to them with reverence. If not, emptiness, like a hungry ghost, will chase us all the days of our life.

After returning from Spain I felt an actual shift in my posture. I see it in my photographs. Like many women playing multiple roles, I was always ready to leap into action. My body poised to fill the next need. After Spain, I started resting back on my heels. I found a new balance point at my core. My family was capable of taking care of things I thought only I could do.

For example, all family communications ran through me. I passed messages from Don to Deb and Doug and from them back to him. Sometimes I was the primary contact point in their relationships. But all that changed when I was not there. It was never clearer than in the first few hours when we were reunited in Spain. After the long flight from Chicago they needed to nap. We rented a cheap room for the day before we left Madrid for other parts of Spain. It had two queen-sized beds.

I walked into the room and flopped on a bed without undressing or pulling down the cover. Then Don flopped across the second bed and was joined by both Doug and Debbie. I was alone. That would not have happened prior to the trip. My role as Mom in the middle was gone. I had learned how to take care of myself.

They learned how to connect without me.

I recently asked my children, who are now in their forties, what they recall about the months of my absence. Doug said, "Marie being frustrated with us." Deb said, "I remember missing you." Then she added, "Mom, it also made me realize that you have a life of your own." My children saw that I am a woman as well as their mother. Women tell me, "I can't live my dreams, but I can help my children live theirs." This is so sad to me. When do we stop deferring to the next generation?

Loved ones need to know our dreams. It's good for them and good for us when they do. Holding onto dreams has far-reaching influence on all relationships and a surprising one on marriages. Dr. John Gottman has been studying marriages for 35 years. He can predict which relationships will make it with 94.6 percent accuracy. He and his wife, Dr. Julie Schwartz Gottman, developed interventions that turn troubled marriages into resilient ones. There are skills couples need to learn.

But when a man asked Gottman if there is one thing that can predict a healthy relationship, he responded "Know your wife's dream." In his book *The Marriage Clinic: A Scientifically Based Marital Therapy*, he writes:

Women usually have been socialized to not honor any dream that is not about relationships. . . . Although they know that they are entitled to develop as autonomous individuals and that any dream is okay to pursue as long as it is consistent with their moral choices, they have been raised to believe that it is selfish and bad to do so. Hence, we find many women who have not individuated to the extent that many men typically have. They need help to honor and hold onto their dreams.

It is dangerous to pay attention to our dreams. It creates waves and stirs up warning voices that are all around and most importantly in our heads. You know the ones I mean? They are the ones that say *don't risk, don't dare the edge.* But those voices are not connected to our souls, but to fear. They are more concerned with our safety, not our satisfaction. Author Anna Quindlen knows this challenge. "Begin to say no to the Greek chorus that thinks it knows the parameters of a happy life when all it knows is the homogenization of human experience. Listen to that small voice from inside you that tells you to go another way."

Listening to that small voice increases awareness. Self-awareness is what brings clarity to our dreams. Focusing on what we want makes many of us uncomfortable. But honoring our dreams has emotional and physical benefits. It adds resilience to relationships. Marital strength requires each partner to honor their own dream and their partner's dream. Daring the edge can help us find our voice. It can also create pain for those we love. Each person in a relationship must answer this question: Just how much can we stretch to let each other become who we long to be?

This winter is another snowy one. But there are no distant places on my agenda. I'm finding more time to look out the window at my garden. Its rhythms help me appreciate life. Soon tender shoots will make their way through the hard earth. Spring will tiptoe in with flirty violets, lilies of the valley, and tender bleeding hearts.

In summer, the bony rose canes that stretch over the front door will be punctuated by crimson dots. Those lingering buds won't hold back their brilliance forever. Soon after their appearance, they'll unwind into ruffled fullness. My garden says to all who will listen, "Life is longing, waiting to unfold."

The same two places still live in me—faithful to family and true to myself. They are in most of us. The tension between them is what makes us aware of what we value. If it were easy we wouldn't appreciate the depth of caring or our desire to be true to our souls. My family has grown to ten people. Doug married Kathy and they gave us Taylor and Reese. Deb married Wes and they added Eliana and Lilly. There are more people to love and be loved by, more people to consider.

Like all of us, I still hear the occasional whispered—*Why not?* Something begins to stir. I start to ask myself—*Why not?* That's when the tugging at my soul starts. That's when it starts for all of us—when we listen. There are unknown worlds in all of us. What we think is the end of the earth is sometimes a rocky shore that can be a starting point. Often it means risking disapproval and even causing pain for others and ourselves.

If we dare pay attention to what it means to be authentic and trust enough to follow it, we'll discover what brings us alive.

Isn't that what we all want?

Violins

Sounding True

*Let the world know you as you are, not as you think you should be, because
sooner or later, if you are posing, you will forget the pose, and then where are you?*
Fanny Brice

*I*s this the call I've been waiting for? Not just waiting for on
this morning, but for years. *This call could change my life,* I
say to myself. It did, but not in ways that I imagined. I look
at the phone and watch as Joe's name appears across the caller ID.
He is a literary agent I met years ago while giving a talk at a local
bookstore. His encouragement to write intrigued me.

My psychotherapy clients have mostly been women. Once we
worked through the issues that brought them to therapy, they often
needed to discover what was next. I designed a daylong workshop called "Dare to Dream" to help women create a future that

inspired them. Frequently they hadn't considered what they *really* wanted to do or even that they had talents that were untapped. I left the private practice part of my career a couple of years ago and concentrated on groups and workshops. That opened time for me to write.

Speaking with women in my office or in small groups was effortless. Translating it to paper was difficult. I relied heavily on quotes from experts and struggled to trust my inner authority. I finished my proposal and submitted it to Joe. Days went by before he called. I could hardly wait to hear his reaction.

Joe's voice sounds friendly yet business-like. He wastes no time getting to the point. "I've read your proposal."

"I have some feedback for you," he continues. "Are you sitting down?"

Here we go—this is just what I was waiting to hear. He has a book deal already. He read my proposal and called one of his many contacts. "They said, 'Joe, grab this woman. We're ready to make an offer.'" OMG! I pull out the stool from under the kitchen island and sit down. My heart pounds as I prepare for the good news.

"Here's the thing Nancy, I think you ought to look for a ghost-writer," he says in a matter-of-fact tone.

Good thing I am sitting down. I am stunned. *He is telling me I am not a writer.* He asked me to sit down because he knew this would be hard to hear. Pop! Energy and excitement escape from my body like air from an inflated balloon.

As his words sink in, my mind races over all that went into completing this proposal. I spent a couple of years attending a writers' group, workshops, and classes. I also spent untold hours of research and writing that filled the fifty-page document he received.

The classes at a local junior college had already delivered a few unsavory messages. One classmate's feedback was particularly harsh.

She peered out at the rest of us from behind a curtain of maroon and midnight colored hair. Her black clothing was accented by a studded dog collar wrapped around her neck. Even her fingernails were black. I swear her teeth were filed to points.

When she read her assignments, they dripped with angst, like blood from a dagger. She dubbed my writing "bubblegum for the soul." I dropped out after a few sessions. If I was going to save any of my minuscule confidence I had to leave.

I was still trying to digest what Joe was saying as he continued to talk. I was upset and distracted. His feedback packed a punch because I trusted his opinion. He paused for a moment and I managed to squeak out, "But I want to write my own book."

"Well you've got your work cut out for you if you do. I have the names of a couple of writing coaches," he offered unenthusiastically. "Also, there just is not enough of you on the page." I wrote down the numbers and said, "I'll call them and get back to you later, Joe." *Really later*, I think to myself…*first I have to lick all the wounds to my ego and dreams.*

At thirteen, sitting in our bedrooms, we wait for something to happen. At sixteen, we get a driver's license and think that might be it. But even after we have the freedom to drive friends and ourselves to countless places, the question returns.

Isn't something big supposed to happen?

But what is that *big thing*?

We search for clues from parents and teachers. No one speaks about the uneasiness that we feel or helps us with these perplexing feelings. There is growing pressure to ignore this inner turmoil and to focus on pleasing others. We get busy constructing our image of an adult life—one that looks like the people we know. We decide that being grownup means behaving like everything is okay even when it's not. *We can do this,* we think. Just like the adults around us, we allow our actions to become less connected to who we truly are.

Our expectation that something is supposed to happen fades.

We settle into our idea of adulthood.

Next, we stop making a critical distinction. We forget that our actions no longer reflect who we are. It is this mistaken identity that lets us believe we are the image rather than our authentic selves. If we peer beneath this image, we'll discover that original question.

Isn't something big supposed to happen?

If we stay curious and have the help of trustworthy others we'll find that Something Big. True adults learn to speak from and maintain a connection to their essence. Intuitively we knew that even before we could put it into words. Because when we reveal our authentic voice we feel alive. We feel real.

That Something Big is finding our true voice.

Most of us experience having our voices squelched rather than encouraged. We are told to *calm down, don't make a scene, don't be too loud,* and *don't be too emotional.* To comply with these messages means a loss of contact with what Eve Ensler, creator of the play *The Vagina Monologues,* calls our "inner girl." Ensler cites a Girls Incorporated study that reveals an increasing demand on girls to please others. Three out of four girl respondents said that they feel pressure to please everyone.

In her book *I Am an Emotional Creature: The Secret Life of Girls Around the World,* Ensler calls for a refocusing of girls' attention from pleasing to daring. Two sentences in the title poem grabbed my attention:

There is a particular way of knowing.
It is like the older women somehow forgot.

There are particular ways of knowing. There is *wisdom* and there is *knowledge*. Knowledge comes from a set of facts. Wisdom comes from the direct experience of living. Our girl selves want to be in direct contact with life.

I am a grandmother of four granddaughters, three of them teenagers. I remember mothering Debbie, our daughter, when she was a teen, and I recall my own teen years. There is a river of intensity running through all of us in adolescence. At times this powerful energy feels unmanageable—to others and to us. Channeling it rather than damming it up is the response that connects us to our voice.

A teenager's energy is often challenging to guide. Their powerful emotions mixed with a desire to experiment with life make older adults shake with concern. As caring adults our role is to learn how to support them without killing their passion. They must learn that to speak boldly doesn't exempt them from having compassion for others. It takes maturity and lots of practice to deliver opinions in a useful way.

The "Goth Girl" in my junior college writing class was looking for a way to express her individuality. Her countercultural attire made that obvious. The intensity of her words demonstrated a lack of concern for others. At least she showed none toward me. Not pleasing others doesn't mean becoming heartless. Looking back from a safe distance, I understand her determination to speak her truth. Everything about Goth Girl said, Don't mess with me. And while her feedback could use some fine tuning, I wish more of us lived by her motto.

Returning to our inner girl can be painful. For many of us, she has been waiting for a long time to speak. She is sad and angry about being ignored. There is enthusiasm, creativity, and daring in our girl selves and with courage we can find her again. I find her when I paint, write, or hang out with friends. For you, it might be backpacking, a protest march, dancing, or speaking up about strongly held beliefs. She can be found anywhere that brings us face to face with life. Passion and intensity are her calling cards.

Still others of us have not forgotten the dynamic part of who they are. Do you know the kind of woman I mean?

She dresses in a style all her own. Her voice—it springs from somewhere deep inside her body. Her laugh starts in her belly and explodes into the room. Even though sometimes you cringe at how she behaves, you love how you feel when you're together.

Occasionally, you do feel embarrassed by her actions—but you always walk away energized. The intensity of girlhood still lives in her. The rules about looking good and pleasing others have been replaced by a bold quirkiness.

She doesn't let the epithet "you're too much" silence her or tamp down her responses. She listens for an inner wisdom to direct her actions. Most of us have experienced our voices emerging from this soulful place. In those times, we've come out of hiding. We may shake with intensity, sob with our truth, or demand to be heard. Our words break forth boldly or tenderly. However it happens, in those moments we fully embody who we are.

We are being true.

Pluck a tuned violin and the other tuned violins in the room will vibrate with that same note. We are like violins when we vibrate with notes of authenticity. Our words invite others to find that place in them. Some would say that it is the heart's voice that connects us to each other. Whatever we call it, we have the ability to resonate with others. Sometimes when we are moved by another's words tears come to our eyes. Yet it isn't sadness we feel. It's gratitude. They have reminded us of who we really are.

I have never played the violin. If I tried it would surely screech. But in the hands of a virtuoso, a violin stirs emotions. A violin's voice becomes throatier, deeper, and richer when played by a skillful musician. It is an exquisite instrument. It transforms. It is said that a violin's wood remembers beautiful notes. The wood and varnish that make up a violin are changed by sound. It is safe, then, to assume that our own voice alters our own flesh and blood. Wouldn't it make sense that the more we speak with authenticity, the truer our lives become?

Sun streams in through the living room windows. Halcyon skies don't match how I feel. Joe's "there just isn't enough of you on the page" comment keeps ringing in my ears. Lost. Confused. I know he is right—but now what? Like a pile of bones, the typed pages of my proposal cover my lap. I comb through them and look for me between the quotes from others and the many factual statements. Mostly the words seem dry and lifeless. They fail to move me.

A familiar voice inside of me shouts, **Give up!**

But then I hear a quiet inner voice whisper, *stay with the struggle. Don't give up. You can do this.*

I pick up the laptop and begin to write.

I came here to speak what I see. Not to convince or persuade but rather to stand firm in my experience—to trust my voice.

This is what I know for sure.

We need to…

Slow Down: to be aware of what is in front of us, around us and within us.

We need to…

Drop In: to be present to our experience while softly and courageously pressing into it.

We need to…

Dare More: by speaking and living the gentle and hard truth of who we are.

Joe's shattering message ripped my professional persona right off my writing. It exposed a truth I'd avoided. I did not trust my own voice to convey the message of the book. Yes, I took him up on the writing coach. I needed skills. But more than skill, I needed to dare to be the woman to write the book—a book with vulnerable me on its pages.

Slowly, I began to listen to my inner longing and to my voice. "A woman must hear the mermaid's song from the sea if she is to make contact with her creative imagination," wrote Helen M. Luke, in *The Way of Woman*. Now my inner girl and the siren's call inform my work.

The time arrives in every woman's life when she knows she must take a risk. Should she leave or should she stay? Does she take that new job or start her own business? Should she trust herself when the world says she is wrong? Will she give up when it looks like she'll fail? Does she make the daring choice?

These are moments when unfolding is at play, when our true self can emerge in a fuller, richer way. More than anything we want to be ourselves. The thought thrills us. It panics us. To trust ourselves we must find that quiet inner voice that whispers in our dreams and thoughts, and in the hunches that pop into our awareness as we drive from errand to errand.

Sadness and fear are often the attendants of these times of growth and change. Lord knows I went through months of upset to find my way back to writing after Joe's call. I cracked open. I unearthed uncertainty and discovered I *could* trust my voice.

Our voices long to be heard.

Some place deep inside of you knows what it needs.

It is ready to tell you.

The question...

Will you listen?

Mirror

Finding Blessings

My mother wanted me to be her wings, to fly as she never quite had the courage to do. I love her for that. I love the fact that she wanted to give birth to her own wings.

Erica Jong

*B*ad luck just shows up.

Blessings have to be found.

My mother's antique silver hand mirror sits on the bathroom vanity along with my hair dryer, brush, creams, makeup, toothbrush, toothpaste, and a scattering of earrings I've worn the last few days. Some people use things and then immediately put them away. Not me. Surfaces must reach a critical mass of objects before they need to be cleared. I operate the same way in the kitchen. When the cake is in the oven I retrace my steps; mop up spills, put things in the dishwasher and return the ingredients to their proper places. Kitchen, desk or bathroom vanity—each receives the same treatment from me.

Sometimes when I pick up my mother's mirror I think about all the years she used it. I wonder what she saw in her reflection. Was she at peace with the face gazing back at her? The mirror was a gift to her from Don and me for watching Debbie and Doug while we took a much needed weekend break. Even though we gave it to her over forty years ago, I still remember that moment. When she died I asked for a few things; a teapot, a cow shaped-creamer, and this mirror.

One obvious problem with my messy countertops is that things crowd together. They begin to perch here and there in precarious ways. That becomes apparent as I reach for the mirror near the hair dryer's tangled cord. I partially connect with its silver handle. This causes the keepsake to flip through the air like a trapeze artist. My empty outstretched hand is helpless to stop it from falling.

I watch in stunned disbelief as the mirror crashes onto the waiting tile floor.

"*OH NO!*" I scream, like a circus audience watching a performer fall to the ground.

Now the mirror lies glass-side down at my feet. The silver side embossed with the face of a chubby cherub surrounded by swirls and flourishes gives no hint as to the condition of the glass. As I turn it over I wonder, if *it is broken will it bring a curse of seven years bad luck? Or will breaking it set me free from the hold that only a mother can have?*

My breath quickens.

Cautiously, I grasp the handle and turn it over.

Phew!

Unbroken.

I clear a secure place and put it back on the countertop as I recommit myself to tidiness, though I know this promise will not last. Then in a whisper I hear my mother say, *Right on Nancy! You've got it girl, keep writing and dipping into the ocean! That is where the mermaids swim and where you'll find your buried treasure.*

Long ago my mother took up residence in my head. Tucked between neurons and ganglia, her messages wait for just the perfect moment to appear. Sometimes her voice supports me. Usually, she urges me to give up, have a snack, and forget about my current project. *It is too hard and the big blue chair in front of the TV is so comfortable,* I hear her whisper. Her communications have a clear reoccurring theme: Avoid any risk or any activities that might create anxiety.

Her habit of avoidance has lessened in me as I have learned to deal with my own fears of risk-taking. But the desire to dodge difficulties still lives within me. Mothers press patterns upon our tender souls. Patterns, like the embossing on this vintage hand mirror. These impressions may diminish over time but they never totally disappear.

Thump

Thump

Thump

From the moment the tiny speck of who we are pulsates with energy we are a unique expression of life. That beat is what you call "you" and what I call "me." From our first heartbeat until our last we are on a journey to protect, nurture, and cherish that throb of life. The patterns of how we were loved or not loved begin at such an early age that they fall beneath our conscious thoughts. They create deep grooves that we tumble into with regularity. Especially when we are stressed, as Barbara Kingsolver puts it in *Homeland and other Stories,* "It's frightening how when the going gets rough you fall back on whatever awful thing you grew up with."

Kingsolver is saying what I've noticed. When I'm upset I often return to how discomfort was addressed in my childhood. Frequently my mother's response was food. It was medicine for any hurt—a cookie for a skinned knee or a doughnut for bruised feelings. We had a silent pact that we would not talk about painful things. So each cookie and doughnut was swallowed with a glass of milk and a generous helping of unexpressed emotions.

My mother lived in a whisper. Quiet. Hidden. There were two exceptions; whistling and singing. Her whistle was an ear-piercing sound. It shot through cornfields, down gravel driveways until our eardrums vibrated with its unmistakable message. *Get home now!*

On laundry days she carried armloads of sheets, my dad's shirts, and our clothes in from the clothesline. They were plopped onto the dining room table before she set up the ironing board and started vanquishing wrinkles. Soon she'd begin singing church hymns and arias from *Madame Butterfly*. I loved listening to her beautiful voice as the iron moved in rhythm to the music. As the hot metal from the iron hit damp cloth, steam rose up around her. She became Madame Butterfly standing in a misty Japanese harbor. Seeing our mothers happy is a wish many children have. It brings a special pleasure.

My father's love was all-encompassing and difficult. His temper was explosive. Why my mother didn't risk speaking up is complex. But to incite anger in loved ones is a step many of us are reluctant to take. She surrendered her dream of being a professional singer in order to live in peace with him. And in the end she neither sang professionally nor lived in peace. Her pattern of dodging conflicts betrayed her.

Most of us are not willing to do the painful work it takes to come back to the true heartbeat of our lives. We seek diversions that direct us away from disturbances. Recreational eating is a common distraction. If we are lucky we discover that no amount of Ben and Jerry's ice cream can take away our turmoil. I know, because I've tried. Repeatedly. There are still times I find myself worshiping at the altar of chocolate, hoping it will help me forget what I feel. At some point, I will give voice to what hurts. But first I am going to eat that *healthy* chocolate bar from Trader Joe's.

Bells of St-Germain-des-Prés clang from the tower above my head. They ring for what seems like a long time, maybe because it is noon on Good Friday. Listening, I sit holding my journal. Seeing London and Paris for the first time with Don is exciting. Being accompanied by our daughter, Debbie, son-in-law Wes, and two of our four granddaughters, Elly, 16, and Lilly, 13, enriches an already enchanting trip.

Working my inner journey while I connect to those I love is always a source of tension. But mostly that angst lives within me. My family is happily exploring other sights. I have come back to the church we visited yesterday. Being here is how I want to spend my last day in Paris.

The woman in front of me sits with her head bowed. She is so still—so quiet. Her fierce focus vibrates like soundless waves that strike my heart. Every muscle and fiber of her being is praying. I imagine she is in pain, the kind that strips away pretense. She doesn't seem to notice anyone else.

Some of us kneel before our plants and gardening becomes our prayer. Writing is my form of reverence. To notice what we really notice—what is all around us and within us—is to be fully alive. It is an act of devotion. Simone Weil, a French philosopher, reflecting on this awareness, said prayer is the act of paying attention. We each pray in our own way.

She who sat and prayed now stands to leave. She bends her knee and touches it to the stone floor. She gestures to her forehead, her chest, and then her left shoulder, followed by the right. It is a sacred sign offered in this ancient church that is said to be built on the foundation of a temple honoring the Goddess Isis. For centuries men and women have gathered on this spot to touch the Great Mystery that appears in many forms. What this women longs for I will never know. But I will always recall the depth of my own longing that she made me remember.

Yearning to understand the invisible world of spirit has been with me for as far back as I can remember. And though my path has been quite different than my mother's, the importance of having a spiritual life is something she demonstrated through her devotion to Christianity. She would not have used my words. But I learned from her that there is an indescribable force running through all of life. I have followed that awareness down many paths.

But what my mother did not teach me could fill a book. She didn't know about living in distant places or painting in a studio until dawn. She didn't know how to drive on busy expressways or find her way around the winding streets of Barcelona. Most importantly, she did not teach me to have a strong voice.

So when I read the following words in Alison Bechdel's book *Are You My Mother?*, I instantly knew what Alison meant. "There was a certain thing I did not get from my mother. There is a lack, a gap, a void. But in its place, she has given me something else. Something, I would argue, that is far more valuable. She has given me the way out." And I can say that also. The way out for me is a spiritual path that lets me sew together the ragged pieces of my soul.

Some would call these gaps *wounds*, a word that has an interesting connection to the word *blessing*. According to Michael Meade, author and scholar, blessing is derived from the French word *blessure,* which is also the origin of the word wound. They are not only related grammatically but together form a truism: Where there is a wound there is also a blessing.

Inside of us is the desire to unfold. The world we were born into also has that as its agenda. To unfold takes tremendous courage, time, and wise support. In the process, we are sure to encounter our own wounds. Whenever I listen to a woman recounting a difficult childhood, I am touched by the pain she has endured, and impressed by her resilience. Often she relied on an inner, unnamable strength. Sometimes a blessing emerged from her ordeal.

Meade says, "If a person isn't at home dwelling near their gifts then they are probably dwelling near their wounds." He is reflecting what I have also seen. Until we work to understand our wounds we will likely live in them and our gifts will remain unclaimed.

It is not surprising that my work supports women as they find and express their voice. It looks obvious from the view of my childhood. One could even say that it was inevitable. However, I did not consciously start this work because of my past. In fact, I did not discover the connection between my mother's failure to speak up and my desire to help women express themselves until years later. My work brings me profound satisfaction. And in the process of helping others, I've become more comfortable with my own voice. Fear and discomfort has not gone away. But they are no longer a reason to give up. They signal that I am moving into uncharted territory.

Finding gifts in the gaps of our childhood includes forgiveness. Forgiveness is giving up the wish that our past could have been any other way. When we stop believing that we ended up in the wrong family with the wrong mother, two important things happen: We see what she did give us and also what we wanted but did not receive from her. "Our problem is not that as children our needs were unmet but that as adults they are still unmourned," David Richo observes in his book *How to Become an Adult*.

There *is* work to do.

We must cry our tears of disappointment. That doesn't mean we give up longing for satisfying care. Mourning done with the awareness that it could not have been any other way releases us to address what we need now. Slowing down and dropping into the present moment, we begin to notice what food makes our bodies sing. We discover we need time alone, days alone, scribbling in journals, quiet walks, eating in silence, hanging out in nature, sitting in ancient churches, and the list goes on when we listen to our soul's longings. It takes work to come home to who we are. And when we do, an inner dwelling place is established that includes both our wounds and our gifts.

From the moment we are born we are evermore a certain child of a certain mother. No two mother-child relationships are the same, not those of siblings, not even twins. We forget this. Each soul has a divine errand to fulfill, and it is played out in all of our relationships.

It is ridiculously hard being a mother. The awareness of the overwhelming demands of mothering can make us more compassionate about the care we ourselves received. Those of us who do step into the shoes of motherhood know just how difficult it is. When you realize that the shift you pulled is 24 hours a day seven days a week, there isn't any pay, and you are ultimately responsible for the emotional and physical well-being of a human life, there is only one reasonable response:

Pitch the idea of being the perfect mother and settle for being a good enough mom.

Nature is the mirror I prefer. Lines and wrinkles are not presented in glaring clarity when I look into that living mirror. Something at my core recognizes itself in nature. I see resilience when the crocuses bloom surrounded by snow. Roses reflect that I unfold one petal at a time. Tinges of red on the burning bush in August remind me that my time here is fleeting. I am soothed watching plants move through their seasons like the rhythmic rocking of a baby. There is something bigger moving in me and around me.

Predictably, my bathroom vanity has again become crowded with sundry toiletries and discarded pieces of jewelry. The silver mirror is still unbroken. When I pick it up I see the face of a woman in her late—really late—sixties who continues to discover how to dive into the gaps and retrieve gifts. Like some spelunking cave diver, I find wonder and fear in these emotional caverns.

I find myself.

I thought mothering would stop at some point, maybe when the kids reached age eighteen, twenty-one, or at least forty. But I see now that it goes on in different forms. I like that. It is clear that while being perfect is what my ego wanted and expected of me, I was not the perfect mother. I was good enough. Each of us who takes on motherhood must come to terms with leaving gaps in the care of their children. Finding the blessings hidden in those gaps—well, that is the work of the children.

It is the work of every soul.

Afterword
You: *Trusting You*

The meditation hall is aglow in golden light from the setting sun. Sounds from a babbling brook and countless birdsongs drift through the open sides of the structure. Hundreds of people sit crossed-legged on the floor. We wait for the arrival of a spiritual teacher. An ornately tufted chair in the front of the room also awaits her.

The women in the hall are dressed in a rainbow of colors. For many of us it is the first time we have draped our bodies in saris. The mavens among us spent time teaching the novices how to do this before we entered the hall. The last time I wrapped my body in yards of fabric was a disaster. It was Halloween. I was in fourth grade and decided that our old curtains would make a wonderful costume. The yards of antique white lace that once adorned our living room windows would be my wedding dress.

I spun the cloth around my body three times, then tucked and pinned it in place. I was now the bride I had always imagined. The big march in and out of other classrooms was rambunctious. The boy behind me was a dragon and had difficulty seeing out of his paper bag headpiece. As we circled through the kindergarten room he stepped on my trailing dress and down it came—nearly to my waist. I was horrified.

I am hoping that doesn't happen again today.

This time, some thirty years later, I feel safely cocooned in nearly five yards of silk shantung. It helps that I am also wearing an under-blouse and slip. It gives me a sense of security. Both were omitted from my childhood dress-designing foray. Excitement in the hall is similar to that fourth grade Halloween day. But it's a lot more orderly. We are silent. Even in the stillness I feel our anticipation.

We close our eyes for meditation. Then a bell rings as a signal to open our eyes. The spiritual teacher has taken her seat before us. She's radiant. Her appearance is more like that of a Vogue model than my idea of an Indian guru. Her thick black hair peeks out from under a tangerine colored pillbox hat. Deep orange cloth lies pleated around her lotus-folded body. Silently she looks at every section of the hall before she speaks. Metaphors and readings from holy books fill her talk as she tells us that it's possible to experience divine consciousness in our human bodies.

Darshan, my favorite part, comes next. Darshan is a Sanskrit word meaning "to see with reverence." I think of it as to behold the teacher and to be held by the teacher with respect. This day we are instructed to ask her an important question. "Ask one that burns inside of you for answer," the MC says. It is an alluring idea. *What do I ask a wise woman,* I wonder. Then I know. I repeat my question over and over as I wait in line. When I reach her I kneel. It is a challenge to do this in a sari. But I do. Then I bow my head. She bops me with a large wand of peacock feathers that smell of sandalwood and myrrh.

I ask my question. She bops me again and says something I barely hear. Rising up unsure of all that just happened I walk away. "Nancy," she calls out. I turn around and look into her eyes as she looks into mine and says these words: "Trust yourself." Clearly. Forcefully. "Trust Yourself."

My meditation cushion of light blue silk marks my place on the floor. It helps me know where to sit when I return to the rows of seated women. I take my seat. Suddenly, my body rocks and shakes. I believe it is the dance of divine energy rushing through me. Even to this day some twenty-five years later, I cannot explain how I felt. Ironically, I don't even remember my question.

It really isn't what's important.

The experience and her response are what is important.

"Trust yourself."

It is also the message at the heart of this book. "Trust Yourself!"

These are my wishes for all of us.

May we be…

Wise enough to welcome what's born through us

Brave enough to shelter it as it grows

Patient enough to honor our process—at every age

Insightful enough to recognize the woman we are already

And daring enough to…

Trust ourselves.

Acknowledgements

While writing *Unfolding* I found my voice—again. Finding our voice is not a destination. It's an ongoing process. At age sixty-eight, I unearthed a place of deeper self-expression.

Unfolding became a reality with the love and support of the following people...

Don Hill, my husband, your undying belief in me, my writing and wisdom, especially when I can't see it, is a priceless gift. Your emotional and financial support made this book possible. Your pure heart illuminates my path.

Doug and Kathy Hill, Debra and Weston Kosova, our children, you're each precious to me and give my life substance. I am deeply grateful to be part of your family.

To our four granddaughters, Eliana, Lillian, Taylor and Reese you continue to open my heart and teach me to see life anew. Watching each of you find your own voices is a blissful journey.

Donna Weltyk you care for this book as though it's your own. Your knowledge of books and research skills enrich my writing and me. You diligently read every word and helped to shape the book. *Unfolding* is a far better book because of you.

Robin Sheerer, your commitment is unwavering. Your laughter helps me find humor in missteps. You have a talent for hearing and pointing out places in writing where something more strains to be heard. Your wise feedback is spot on and made me a better writer.

Monica Rix Paxson, your strength and determination mixed with a wicked sense of humor and a laser-like mind never lets me hide. You push me to think with rigor and write with confidence.

Women of the women's circles, past and present, your courageous truth-telling inspires me. You continue to demonstrate that a circle of committed compassionate woman can find blessings in wounds and strength in speaking. Your names are written upon my heart.

Joe Durepos your insistence that I had something worth contributing along with a dose of tough love made me a better writer and a stronger woman.

Cindy Crosby you recognized my true voice before I did, then helped me uncover it. A writing coach can offer no greater gift.

Laura Jane Murphy and Yoga Among Friends community your loving arms hold me in countless ways. All is possible in your embrace.

Oriah Mountain Dreamer your generosity and wise words move me to tears. I'm proud to call you my teacher, confidante, and friend.

Cathy Williams you brought White Cloud Press to me. I'm forever grateful for that along with our friendship.

Michelle Cassou, you teach with fierce compassion and taught me to trust the creative process.

Rich Lessor, your steadfast council always makes the choice clear—it's either fear or love.

Steve Scholl and White Cloud Press thank you for believing in me and my writing. There is a special place in heaven for publishers like you.

Christy Collins, you took my words and turned them into a book. Your gracious spirit, dedicated work, and creativity made this project easier than it might have been. Thank you!

Finally, to that whimsical mermaid who flirted with my soul and took me on this remarkable journey, you're now a part of me.

Perhaps you always were.

Discussion Questions

In the introduction, **Doorways: Entering the Mystery,** Nancy Hill says, "There are women who came before, sat to write, stood to paint, stretched to dance, cleared their throats, and spoke." Who are the women who have inspired you?

1. **Hummingbirds: Tugging on Invisible Cords.** "But the longer I live the more I realize this obvious truth: I am not in charge." The placement of the hummingbird feeder showed Hill how she likes being in control. Nature is often a great teacher. What lessons have you learned from observing the natural world?

2. **Mermaid: Soul Spotting.** Nancy Hill talks about two parts inside of her. The file clerk, or rational mind, likes to maintain the status quo. But her soul favors following her heart. Have you ever felt these conflicting tugs? What might happen if you began to follow your intuitive hunches? Would slowing down help you hear intuition's whispers? Does her fascination with the mermaid puzzle or delight you?

3. **Moon: Remembering Essence.** What does waking up to your life, mean to you? Nancy says, "The roles we play are similar to the phases of the moon." When have your roles obscured the essence of who you are? Does being in nature help you return to your core self?

4. **Red Pepper: Be Here Now.** "We begin to confuse labeling with knowing." Nancy is telling us we miss so much because we quickly dismiss what we see. How might your life be different if you looked deeply into your own eyes? What might you learn about you?

5. **Bees: Savoring Senses.** Nancy is telling us that paying attention to the senses brings us into the present moment. Do you have a practice like journaling, cooking, gardening, or something else that helps you slow down and become aware of the senses?

6. **Bananas: Tending the Sparks.** "The question isn't, *Am I creative?* The question is, *Do I recognize it? Do I nurture it?* Where does the creative spark appear in your life? What do you experience when you hear the word creativity. Fear? Excitement?

7. **Hag: Embracing What's Real.** What does it mean to have a voice? A woman's voice? What does that mean to you? What in this book has helped you uncover your voice?

8. **Tootsie Pop: Reaching Our Core.** "Finding our voice isn't an esoteric pursuit but an essential human endeavor." How would you define core self? What is it about the second half of a woman's life that makes that core self easier to find?

9. **Noxzema Jars: Cracking Open.** "Our authenticity depends on how we meet these moments." What difficulties in your life have introduced you to a deeper sense of you?

    Job loss? Death of a loved one? Health issues? Ending a relationship?

10. **Penguin: Holding On.** Where do we place our faith? What things—books, ideas or beliefs sustain you during difficult times? Do you have a certain book that you like to read and reread?

11. **Mountains: Living in Layers.** Rediscovering what's hidden. Are there aspects of you that were left behind and that you later rediscovered?

12. **Dish Soap: Tumbling Awake.** The ability to know others is a gift. Knowing who we are—a necessity. How does what we believe about ourselves color how others treat us?

13. **Hot Coffee: Ignoring the Muse.** Inspiration connects us to our souls. "It's an invitation to cooperate in our own unfolding process." How do you measure what's important to complete in a day?

14 **Gypsy: Daring the Edge.** Faithful to our families—true to us—the dance of every caring person. Do you experience a pull between turning within and connecting with others? Do you make sure that you have time by yourself? Daily? Weekly?

15. **Violins: Sounding True.** It requires mining vulnerability and voice. In what parts of your life do you experience your "girl self?" Backpacking? Dancing? Being with friends? Painting? Writing? Walking in the woods?

16. **Mirror: Finding Blessings.** Letting go of the hoped for a different childhood and finding blessings in our wounds. Is

there something you wished for as a child that you now give to yourself? Nurturance? Self-acceptance? When you look at the gaps or wounds of your childhood do you also see strengths that grew out of those experiences?

Afterword. You: Trusting You. Nancy urges us to trust ourselves. In what ways are you learning to trust yourself?

Reading List

Ackerman, Diane. *A Natural History of the Senses* (New York: Random House, 1990).

Barks, Coleman. *The Essential Rumi* (San Francisco, CA: Harper, 1995).

Bohm, David, and Donald Factor. *Unfolding Meaning: A Weekend of Dialogue with David Bohm* (London: Routledge, 1995).

Campbell, Joseph, Joseph Campbell, Bill D. Moyers, and Bill D. Moyers. *The Power of Myth* (New York: Doubleday, 1988).

Cassou, Michele. *Point Zero: Creativity Without Limits* (New York: Jeremy P. Tarcher/Putnam, 2001).

Chödrön, Pema. *When Things Fall Apart: Heart Advice for Difficult Times* (Boston: Shambhala, 1997).

Chödrön, Pema, and Sandy Boucher. *Taking the Leap: Freeing Ourselves from Old Habits and Fears* (Boston, Mass.: Shambhala Publications, Inc., 2009).

Crosby, Cindy. *Waiting for Morning: Hearing God's Voice in the Darkness* (Grand Rapids, Mich.: BakerBooks, 2001).

———— *By Willoway Brook: Exploring the Landscape of Prayer* (Brewster, Mass.: Paraclete Press, 2003).

Dillard, Annie. *Pilgrim at Tinker Creek; An American Childhood; The Writing Life* (New York: Quality Paperback Book Club, 1990).

Estes, Clarissa Pinkola. *Women Who Run with the Wolves: Myths and Stories of the Wild Woman Archetype* (New York: Ballantine Books, 1992).

Frankl, Viktor E. *Man's Search for Meaning* (Boston: Beacon Press, 2006).

Friedan, Betty. *The Feminine Mystique* (New York: W.W. Norton, 1963).

Gilligan, Carol. *In a Different Voice: Psychological Theory and Women's Development* (Cambridge, Mass.: Harvard University Press, 1982).

Hollis, James. *The Middle Passage from Misery to Meaning in Midlife* (Toronto: Inner City Books, 1993).

————*Finding Meaning in the Second Half of Life: How to Finally Really Grow Up* (New York: Gotham Books, 2005).

Johnson, Robert A. *Owning Your Own Shadow: Understanding the Dark Side of the Psyche* (San Francisco: Harper San Francisco, 1991).

————*Inner Gold: Understanding Psychological Projection* (Kihei, Hawaii: Koa Books, 2008).

Ladinsky, Daniel James. *The Subject Tonight Is Love: 60 Wild and Sweet Poems* (New York: Penguin Compass, 2003).

Lamott, Anne. *Bird by Bird: Some Instructions on Writing and Life* (New York: Anchor Books, 1995).

————*Plan B: Further Thoughts on Faith* (New York: Riverhead Books, 2005).

Lindbergh, Anne Morrow, and Carl H. Pforzheimer. *Gift from the Sea* (New York: Pantheon, 1955.

May, Gerald G. *The Awakened Heart: Opening Yourself to the Love You Need* (San Francisco: Harper San Francisco, 1993).

Mountain Dreamer, Oriah. *The Invitation* (San Francisco: Harper San Francisco, 1999).

————*What We Ache For: Creativity and the Unfolding of Your Soul* (San Francisco: Harper San Francisco, 2005).

Muir, John. *Nature Writings: The Story of My Boyhood and Youth; My first Summer in the Sierra; The Mountains of California; Stickeen; Selected Essays* (New York: Literary Classics of the United States, 1997).

Oliver, Mary. *New and Selected Poems, Vol. 1* (Boston: Beacon Press, 1st edition).

Pearce, Joseph Chilton. *The Crack in the Cosmic Egg; Challenging Constructs of Mind and Reality* (New York: Julian Press, 1971).

————*Evolution's End: Claiming the Potential of Our Intelligence* (San Francisco: Harper San Francisco, 1992).

Richo, David. *Shadow Dance: Liberating the Power and Creativity of Your Dark Side* (Boston, MA: Shambhala, 1999).

————*Being True to Life: Poetic Paths to Personal Growth* (Boston: Shambhala, 2009).

Rilke, Rainer Maria, and Robert Bly. *Selected Poems of Rainer Maria Rilke* (New York: Harper & Row, 1981).

Shlain, Leonard. *The Alphabet Versus the Goddess: The Conflict Between Word and Image* (New York: Penguin, 1999).

Taylor, Barbara Brown. *An Altar in the World: A Geography of Faith* (New York: Harper One, 2009).

Whyte, David. *The Heart Aroused: Poetry and the Preservation of the Soul in Corporate America* (Crown Business; Reissue edition, June 1, 1996).